Instructor's Guide
for
Choices, Challenges, Changes and *More Choices*

by

Judy Edmondson, Mindy Bingham, Sandy Stryker,
Sue Fajen, Michele Jackman, Kathleen Peters, Penelope C. Paine and Lari Quinn

Edited by
Barbara B. Greene and Kathleen Peters

ISBN 0-911655-04-2

Published by Advocacy Press • P.O. Box 236 • Santa Barbara, California 93102

Printed in the United States of America

The first edition of the Instructor's Guide was made possible by a grant from Chevron U.S.A. Inc.

The Most Effective Life Planning Courses Available Today

Use *Choices* and *Challenges* in:

Junior High/High School

- Career Education
- Home Economics
- Counseling Settings
- Pregnant Teen Programs
- Young Mother Programs
- Drop-out Prevention Programs
- English and Social Studies
- Teen Pregnancy Prevention

Use *More Choices* in:

High School and College Re-entry

- Home Economics
- Career Development Classes
- Consumer Math/Economics
- Vocational Readiness Programs
- Displaced Homemaker Programs
- Parenting/Family Life Programs
- Gifted Student Programs
- Teen Parent Programs

Use *Changes* in:

- College Re-entry
- Displaced Homemaker Programs
- Re-entry Programs
- Vocational Readiness Programs
- Individual Counseling
- Career and Life Planning Classes

Foreword

Choices, Challenges, Changes, More Choices: People of both sexes and all ages face them every day, like it or not. Your job, and ours, is to make sure that every student in your class comes away with the improved skills and increased understanding he or she needs to make the best decisions.

You will accomplish this not by lecturing, but by leading . . . by listening . . . by encouraging your students to express their ideas, feelings, and opinions . . . and by lending caring support as they come to grips with themselves, their relationships, and their futures.

This combined *Instructor's Guide* attempts to make your job easier, no matter which course you are teaching. *Choices* is designed to work side by side with either *Challenges* or *Changes,* although some subjects differ. These books are meant primarily for students who have not given much thought to their future careers. *More Choices* is designed for students who are already aware of their need to prepare for a career.

But you are likely to find materials from all the books valuable. Perhaps your *More Choices* students will need to brush up on some of the basic skills covered in the other three books, or they might find Chapter 7 in *Changes* helpful. Similarly, the materials from *More Choices* can be used to illustrate how the topics in *Choices, Challenges,* and/or *Changes* are pertinent to any student hoping to combine career and family life.

This *Instructor's Guide* takes you through the exercises in all four books, shows you how to use them in different combinations, and offers cross-references to related topics. It sets out the goals and objectives for each chapter clearly, and explains how to deal with the differences in the texts if you are conducting a *Choices/Challenges* class. In addition, you will find information on using the texts in different settings (math or English classes, for example), class organization plans, discussion outlines, and guidance on outside speakers and class extension ideas.

These classes can be emotional experiences for students who are just beginning to explore, question and reshape their assumptions about the world and about themselves. The most difficult part of your job may be to remain neutral as you encourage them to weigh the consequences of their actions and to make new decisions for themselves. You will enjoy cheering them on and reinforcing their feelings of increased self-confidence and control.

Go to it . . . have fun . . . and good luck!

Contents

Some Background

It all started the day a young, single mother came to the Girls Incorporated Center in tears because she couldn't afford to pay her rent and feed her two children properly. "Why didn't someone tell me what it would be like when I grew up?" she cried. Her pleading question made real what we already knew, at least in an abstract sense: that millions of mothers and children in this country are living in or near poverty. A major cause of this unacceptable fate is that young women-women who are still in school and have yet to make major life-altering choices-have not been convinced by a traditional education that they need to prepare for a career that could adequately support them and their children. They still believe that someone else will take care of them.

In reality, however, 90 percent of American women will work for an average of 25-45 years. Two-thirds of them will work because they must, often because they desperately need the money. They may be divorced (50 percent of marriages end this way, and many men do not pay alimony), they may never have married, they may need to supplement their husbands' income in order to make ends meet, or they may need to support the family if their husbands are unable to work.

Choices was written to convince young women that career education is as important to them as it is to brothers and boyfriends. Without a good job (and that usually means a job requiring some kind of training, possibly one held most often by men), they are in grave danger of entering the overcrowded ranks of those living on welfare, in poverty, and in desperation.

We strongly believe that, in order to overcome the Cinderella fantasies that still plague young women, it is important to begin a career-awareness program early, while teens are just beginning to make the decisions that will have an impact on their futures. Before young women can be expected to make wise career decisions, they must be convinced that they need to know how to support themselves. This is one major difference between career education for young women and young men. The boys generally have already accepted the fact that their adult years will be spent in the workforce.

We wrote *Choices* with this difference in mind. The problem then became how to reach large numbers of young women, young women who are unlikely to buy the book, even if they can afford it. And so we turned to the schools. Testing the materials there showed that, with the help of a teacher, students could make great strides in learning, and many students could benefit.

As soon as *Choices* began to circulate, however, a new need became apparent: Boys, too, needed to learn the skills *Choices* teaches. We thought at first that young men could use the same text, but this began to seem unfair. Although 75 percent of the material in *Choices* is equally useful to both sexes, there are areas in which young men and young women have very different needs. While boys do not usually need to be motivated to prepare for a career, for example, they do need to be made aware of the rapidly changing society they will soon enter.

Consequently, *Challenges* was published as a parallel to *Choices*. The two companion books can be used simultaneously in a coed class.

At this point, we thought our job was done. Once again, we were proved wrong. We heard from many adult women that they, too, needed to learn the skills taught in *Choices* and *Challenges*. They needed them especially if they were about to re-enter the workforce, perhaps after many years at home. We also began to note studies showing that parents' attitudes are often a deciding factor in the career choices of their children.

We began to experiment with mother-daughter programs in which parent and child worked through the exercises in *Choices* together. For most of the exercises, this worked very well. But there were some obvious problems. Mothers do not need to spend a week with a decorated egg (The Egg and You exercise) in order to learn about the difficulties of parenting, for example.

What these women are often facing — and what *Choices* does not touch on — is the process of change. So, by editing most chapters and replacing the old Chapter 7 with a whole section on change, we developed *Changes,* a basic program for adult women. It can be used on its own, or in conjunction with *Choices* in mother-daughter programs. (See the Mother-Daughter Choices section in this book.)

More Choices builds on the topics of the other books and goes a step beyond. While the earlier texts point out that their readers are likely to have both jobs and families, they do not address the obvious question: How can a set of parents — or, more difficult still, single parents hold down jobs, raise children, care for their homes and their relationships, and still have time to eat, sleep, and maybe even read a newspaper or go to a movie?

As we traveled around the country, we saw that this is one of the most prevalent questions of our day. We began to read about it, think about it and discuss our ideas. And we put our best answers into this book. Eventually, society will change to make life easier for working parents. But, until then, the material in *More Choices* should help.

With pre-career awareness training from *Choices, Challenges* or *Changes,* followed by information in career and life planning from *More Choices,* students should be prepared to go after the kind of life they will find most fulfilling.

It is our fervent hope:

- That students of both sexes will come to accept the concept of equal partnership in marriage.
- That young women will give serious thought to their career choice.
- That young men will be more attentive to their relationships.
- That all students will learn to live a balanced life.
- That no one need sacrifice career for the sake of family, or family for the sake of career.
- That with knowledge and planning all people are empowered to live the life of their choosing.

We encourage you to review the books. They may be ordered through Advocacy Press, P.O. Box 236, Santa Barbara, CA 93102. (805) 962-2728.

How to Use the Books

While the books stand alone and have individual value, they also work together to comprise a comprehensive training course on career and life planning.

As we have noted elsewhere, *Choices, Challenges* and *Changes* deal with the basic planning skills: goal setting, decision making, values identification, career research and so on. We suggest you use them as follows:

- *Choices* **alone** for classes of young women.
- *Challenges* **alone** for groups of young men.
- *Choices* and *Challenges* **together** for coed classes.
- *Changes* **alone** for groups of adult women.
- *Choices* and *Changes* **together** for mother-daughter programs

More Choices covers more advanced topics in career and life planning. Groups or individuals with a firm grasp of basic planning skills may go directly to this volume. Or, it is a logical next step for:

- Young men and women who have completed the *Choices/Challenges* curriculum.
- Adults trying to balance career and family life after completing the *Changes* curriculum.
- Women who have completed the *Choices/Challenges* Mother-Daughter program.

The books can be incorporated into any of the following:

Career Education
Home Economics
Counseling
Pregnant Teen Programs
Young Mother Programs
Drop-Out Prevention Programs
English and Social Studies
Teen Pregnancy Prevention
Life Planning Classes
Vocational Readiness Programs
Displaced Homemaker Programs
Parenting/Family Life Programs
Gifted Student Programs
Mathematics
Re-entry Programs

Song of the Day

As a motivational tool, playing a current or past hit song may help get the class off to a good start. Music can be energizing and serve as a cultural example.

We suggest you use the "Song of the Day" in the following manner. Start playing the song about three minutes before the period is to begin so that as students walk into the room, they can discuss the messages being given. Then, *just* as the bell rings and all students take their seats, begin the recording again so everyone has a chance to hear the entire song. When the song is over, introduce your topic for the day and ask how the message the song presented relates to that subject. This should only take the first two or three minutes of class. Do not dwell on the recording, although you may want to refer to it later if appropriate.

Music is a major part of our culture, especially for teens. This exercise will reinforce learning later, when your students hear the songs played again, and will also help them learn to discern the messages they are receiving, in many cases subconsciously, from this medium. This is important because messages delivered through music for teens today are often negative and even self-destructive.

If you choose to use this as part of your lesson plan, you will probably need to get songs from a wide variety of sources. Start with your own music collection and those of your friends and colleagues. Ask your students to bring in selections. Or, ask for help from the other students in your school.

We have attempted to choose a sample of recordings that have messages about the topics covered in the curriculum. We'd like to hear from you as you find suitable suggestions for the Song of the Day. Please send your ideas to Advocacy Press.

Songs for *Choices* and *Challenges*

Current Hits	Artist/Source	Subject Matter
"Believe"	Lenny Kravitz	Self Esteem/Motivational
"I Will Not Take These Things for Granted"	Toad the Wet Sprocket	Positive Direction
"Streets of Philadelphia"	Bruce Springsteen	Vulnerability
"Control"	Janet Jackson	Assertiveness
"Depend on Me"	Bryan Adams	Vulnerability
"Under the Bridge"	Red Hot Chili Peppers	Making a Change
"Don't Look Back"	Fine Young Cannibals	Motivational
"I Don't Want to Fight"	Tina Turner	Assertiveness
"Stand"	R.E.M.	Motivational
"Heat on the Street"	Phil Collins	Goal Setting
"Greatest Love"	Whitney Houston	Motivational Message
"Right Now"	Van Halen	Motivational
"Mama Help Me"	Edie Brickell & New Bohemians	Vulnerability
"Pride (In the Name of Love)"	U2	Positive Direction
"One Bright Day"	Ziggy Marley & the Melody Makers	Positive Direction
"Don't Walk Away"	Bad English	Assertiveness
"Walking in My Shoes"	Depeche Mode	Different Point of View
"Change"	Tears for Fears	Motivational Message
"Winds Beneath my Wings"	Bette Midler	Inspiration
"Let's Wait Awhile"	Janet Jackson	Vulnerability
"When the Going Gets Tough"	Billy Ocean	Motivational Message

Classics (Older Hits)	Artist/Source	Subject Matter
"Lady Madonna"	The Beatles	Beginning (Chap. 3)
"Three Little Birds"	Bob Marley & The Wailers	Positive Message
"We Don't Need No Education"	Pink Floyd	Negative Media Message
"Lean on Me"	Club Nouveau	Unplanned Pregnancy
"What a Feeling"	Irene Cara	Risk Taking
"Cat's in the Cradle"	Harry Chapin	Males (Chap. 2)
"Nine to Five"	Dolly Parton	Women in the Work Force
"Girls Just Wanna Have Fun"	Cyndi Lauper	Negative Media Message
"Break My Stride"	Matthew Wilder	Superman/Superwoman Syndrome
"Future's So Bright"	Tim Buk 3	Positive Direction (Chap. 10)
"Love Child"	Diana Ross	Pregnancy Prevention
"She's Leaving Home"	The Beatles	Teen Pregnancy
"Ob La Di Ob La Da"	The Beatles	Working - Average Family
"Stand by Your Man"	Tammy Wynette	Traditional Roles

Songs for *More Choices*

Title	Artist	Subject Matter
"Daydream Believer"	The Monkees or Anne Murray	Happily Ever After
"Happy End"	Judy Collins	Happily Ever After
"Some Folks Lives Roll Easy"	Paul Simon	Reality
"The River"	Bruce Springsteen	Reality
"Nine to Five"	Dolly Parton	Working Women
"Sisters Are Doing It for Themselves"	Arethea Franklin	Working Women
"D-I-V-O-R-C-E"	Tammy Wynette	Divorce
"Money"	The Beatles	Money
"Can't Buy the Love"	The Beatles	Money
"Who Wants to be a Millionaire?"	From *High Society*	Money
"Money Changes Everything"	Cyndi Lauper	Income
"If I Were a Rich Man"	From *Fiddler on the Roof*	Income
"Anything Goes"	Cole Porter	Values
"Slip Slidin' Away"	Paul Simon	Time
"I'm Gonna Be an Engineer"	Peggy Seeger	Professional
"Paperback Writer"	The Beatles	Free-lance
"Keep the Customer Satisfied"	Paul Simon	Salesperson
"The Boy in the Bubble"	Paul Simon	Technology
"Working on the Highway"	Bruce Springsteen	Blue Collar
"I Can Do That"	From *A Chorus Line*	Competence
"Climb Every Mountain"	From *The Sound of Music*	Commitment to a Goal
"I Whistle a Happy Time"	From *The King and I*	Confidence
"Everybody Says Don't"	Stephen Sondheim	Courage
"When Numbers Get Serious"	Paul Simon	Math
"Crazy Love, Vol II"	Paul Simon	Today's Varied Relationships
"That's What Friends Are For"	Dionne Warwick	Dual-Income Households
"Old Friends"	Simon and Garfunkel	Friends
"It's Not My Cross to Bear"	Allman Brothers	Friends
"Whipping Post"	Allman Brothers	Stress
"Turn Around"	From *Fiddler on the Roof*	Full-Time Parenting
"Inch by Inch"	Pete Seeger	Planning
"We Are the World"	Lionel Richie/Michael Jackson	Making the World a Better Place
"Blowin' in the Wind"	Bob Dylan	Making the World a Better Place

Before You Begin

Your *Instructor's Guide* is meant to be just that — a guide. The curriculum is extremely flexible and may be used in classes conducted from six weeks to a year. The most common formats in school settings are nine-week quarters or eighteen-week semesters. As there is no "right way," feel free to pick and choose those ideas and suggestions appropriate for you and your students' needs.

This guide is developed by book, by chapters, and then by individual exercises within each chapter. Each exercise contains a learning objective, presentation suggestions, and, when appropriate, suggestions for additional activities, follow-up, and resources. You will find a picture of the cover of each book containing that exercise at the top of the page. Suggestions from instructors across the country are noted.

Following the curricula, we have included information on different programs using the books. Other sections include working with teens, group dynamics and classroom techniques. You may wish to refer to these sections during the course of your program. At the end of this guide, you will also find sections on community resources, how to start a program in your community, and training opportunities available.

One comment should be made before you begin. Classroom discussions are an important part of these classes. To stimulate lively discussions, a supportive, caring environment is essential. Physical situations conducive to good discussion are those in which all members of the class can see each other. Thus desks or chairs arranged in a circle, or seats around tables, are preferable to desks arranged in rows.

Guidelines for discussions should be established at the beginning of the class. These should include such simple statements as the following:

1. Each person is entitled to be heard and to express a personal opinion.
2. A student may not interrupt, ridicule or discount another student's opinion.

Sometimes it may become appropriate to discuss controversial or emotional topics in class, at the discretion of the teacher. At other times, a student may indicate during a discussion that the subject is a serious personal problem. If such circumstances arise, the teacher needs to be aware of agencies or individuals who might be a source of assistance. The teacher should make such resource information available in such a way that the student receives the suggestion as a choice, and not an indication that there is "something wrong" with him or her. A possible statement might be, "I have a list of local agencies and individuals that are experts in providing information or guidance that you might find helpful." Showing genuine concern in a warm and accepting tone of voice is almost always appreciated.

If a student seems to be upset, make a point to "touch base" after class. It's helpful if you have a time each day when students can see you if they wish. If students seem to approach emotional areas that are too delicate for **your** setting, a comment on your part that confirms what they are feeling and then moves the conversation back to a less intense level can be very helpful. For example, if a student brings up a painful experience with an intoxicated parent, you would acknowledge what the student feels and say, "That must have been very frightening for you." Then, move on to a lighter level by making a general statement about the problems alcohol causes for many families. Acknowledging the problems and feelings associated with the situation tells the individual, "I hear what you are saying and I care about you." The result is often significant relief for the student.

We'd Like to Hear from You!

As you teach the class, you will probably find many ideas that work well, and you may have some observations on problems that occur. As you discover resources (films, videos and publications) we would like to hear about them and how you used them. We would appreciate hearing your thoughts and ideas, so we can share them with others, both in future editions and in training sessions.

Our address is:

Advocacy Press
P.O. Box 236
Santa Barbara, CA 93102
(805) 962-2728
1-800-676-1480
FAX: (805) 963-3580

Challenges:
A Young Man's Journal for
Self-awareness and Personal Planning
Choices:
A Teen Woman's Journal for
Self-awareness and Personal Planning
by Mindy Bingham, Judy Edmondson, and Sandy Stryker

Choices and Challenges Curriculum

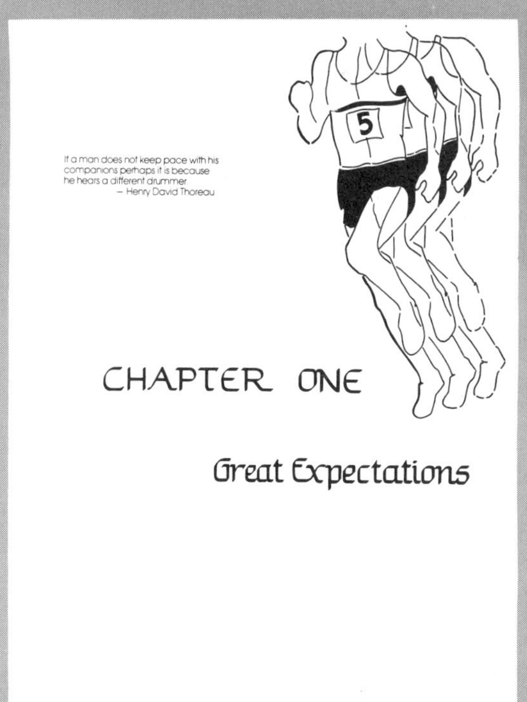

Chapter One

Chapter One is an introduction to both books. It asks readers to think about their futures and examine their attitudes toward the relationship between work and sex-role stereotyping. All readers should feel free to choose from the whole range of possible life options. Preconceived notions about the suitability of careers are self-limiting for both young men and women.

Envision Your Life

PAGE 13 **Workbook 4**

Objectives:

1. To stimulate students to begin thinking about their futures and practice stretching their imaginations.
2. To provide the teacher with some insight as to student perceptions at the start of the class.

Presentation Suggestions:

This exercise works well when the teacher or leader prepares a large chart using his or her own life as an example. As students watch the teacher complete a personal chart in class, they gain ideas for their own charts.

Another way to help students think about the future is to ask them to think of a friend, someone they know very well. Have them imagine they are editors of a yearbook, and their job is to make predictions about people. Ask, "What can you see your friend doing five years from now?" Most students have little trouble figuring out the directions their friends are heading. Then ask, "What would you like someone to write about you?"

Activities:

Ask students to fill in a similar chart for a famous person from the past or a familiar person in their own lives, such as a grandmother or relative. Then they can complete their own.

Follow-Up:

The exercise can be repeated at the end of the course as students reexamine their goals and plans. Note any changes.

Post-Test:

This is an ideal post-test to be given at the end of the course. By comparing the students' first charts completed at the beginning of the course with their post-test charts, you can evaluate the growth the students experienced because of the class. Are their new plans more realistic and better thought out? Do they see more options in their lives? Was the post-test easier to fill out and more complete?

Attitude Inventory

PAGES 14-15 **Workbook 5-6**

Objective:

To encourage students to examine their attitudes about sex roles.

Presentation Suggestions:

A good film to spark a discussion of this topic is "Making Points," produced by Girls Incorporated. In the film, teenage boys on a basketball court are interviewed about their ideas, feelings, and views of their roles in life. The comments they make in the film were actually all made by teenage girls in group interviews, and it is eye-opening and amusing to hear the remarks coming out of the mouths of boys. Well done and short, the film sparks lively discussions. Following the film, students complete the "Attitude Inventory" for a closer look at their own opinions. Stress that responses are not necessarily right or wrong, but that individuals should be prepared to defend their points of view.

Activities:

This is a good point for a discussion of sex-role stereotyping. You might read your students the following definition of "stereotype" from the *American Heritage Dictionary*:

"A stereotype is a person, group, event, or issue considered to typify or conform to an unvarying pattern or manner, lacking any individuality."

Do your students know two people who are exactly alike? If there aren't even two people just like each other, does it make sense that half the population of the world can be said to fit into a predetermined mold? How does it make them feel to be considered to be "lacking any individuality"?

Another activity would be to ask students the question asked in the survey by Dr. Alice Baumgartner: "How would your life be different if you'd been born a boy/girl?" Then read aloud the article in Redbook (see Resources) which looks at and analyzes the responses of 2,000 students in Colorado. Since the study finds a "fundamental contempt for females" by both sexes, this article leads to interesting discussions. Student responses in your classes can also be compared with the survey responses.

"X: A Fabulous Child's Story," by Lois Gould, is a humorous story that presents the idea of raising a nonsexist child by not letting anyone know the child's sex. The story reads well aloud and sparks discussion. Or you may ask students to write an essay about their reactions.

Energizer:

Use the center aisle of the classroom to make an imaginary graph. At one end is the point *strongly agree;* at the other end is *strongly disagree.* The center would represent *undecided.* Read a statement from the inventory aloud, and have students move to the position in the classroom that represents their opinions (i.e. *agree, disagree* or *undecided).* The leader can then ask for volunteers from opposing sides to discuss their choices. Students may change their places along the imaginary graph at any time during this discussion if they hear something that changes their mind. Another alternative is to have the students with opposing opinions talk to each other.

"Making Points," a film that presents a powerful look at sex-role stereotyping in an amusing and entertaining way, is available from:

Direct Cinema Ltd., P.O. Box 315, Franklin Lakes, New Jersey 07417. (201) 891-8240 or P.O. Box 69799, Los Angeles, CA 90069

Resources:

Carson, Dale. *Girls Are Equal Too: The Women's Movement for Teenagers.* New York: Atheneum, 1973.

Gould, Lois and Maggie Tripp, ed. "X: A Fabulous Child's Story," *Women in the Year 2,000.* New York: Arbor House, 1974.

Tavris, Carol, with Alice I. Baumgartner. "How Would Your Life Be Different If You'd Been Born a Boy?" *Redbook,* February 1983.

Your Family

PAGES 16-18 **Workbook 7-9**

Objectives:

1. To examine verbal and nonverbal message families give to their members.
2. To evaluate how these messages affect attitudes about future options.
3. To note any difference between messages to boys and messages to girls.

Presentation Suggestions:

Discuss the messages young people most commonly receive from the family. Divide the students into dyads to discuss the topic. This stimulates thought and helps students learn to feel comfortable with each other.

The different messages given to boys and girls could be examined in terms of:

a. Toys given.

b. Play activities encouraged.

c. Privileges and freedoms.

Ask students to bring toys to class, or bring them yourself. Discuss the differences between "girls'" toys and "boys'" toys.

Then ask students to complete the exercise on pp. 16-17. *Choices* and *Challenges* present differing messages to examine.

Choices	***Challenges***
Success in school	"Being a man"
Appearance	Work
Marriage	Success
Career	Relationship/Marriage
Children	Expressing emotion

Activities:

A panel of parents could visit the class to discuss raising nonsexist children.

Follow-Up:

After the discussion, complete the exercise, "Messages You Would Give Your Daughter/Son," on p.18. This allows the students to internalize the learning. If they experienced any growth toward change during this discussion, it would be reflected here.

Resources:

Eastman, Raisa. *A Portrait of American Mothers & Daughters.* Pasadena: NewSage Press, 1987. (P.O. Box 41029, Pasadena, CA 91114.)

Bridge the Generation Gap

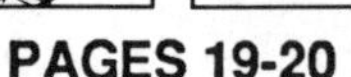

Workbook 11

Objective:

To encourage students to communicate with people close to them who influence their attitudes.

Presentation Suggestions:

Review simple interview techniques in class. These will be useful in future exercises and later in life when students need to gather information.

They include:

1. Be polite and respectful so that people will want to talk to you.
2. Don't impose your attitudes on the person being interviewed. Avoid questions that begin with phrases like, "Don't you agree that . . . ?"
3. Let the other person do most of the talking.
4. Ask questions that encourage the person to talk. Such questions usually begin with "why" or "how" or "what do you think?" Avoid questions that can be answered simply "yes" or "no

After reviewing the listed questions in class, discuss any other questions the group might like to ask.

Assign the exercise as homework.

Follow-Up:

Once the class completes the assignment, ask students to share some of their interviews.

Are any themes running throughout the interview responses? For example, did women working outside the home answer differently from homemakers? How did men differ from women in their responses?

Have You Ever Met a Woman Truck Driver?

Have You Ever Met a Male Nurse?

PAGE 21 Workbook 12

Objective:

To make students aware of the subconscious associations of gender with jobs, based on what they see around them.

Presentation Suggestions:

Ask students if there is any job a woman can't do. Is there any job a man can't do? If so, what? What is it about a woman/man that makes it impossible for her/him to do this job?

Activities:

As a class, think of jobs closely associated with one sex. List reasons why these jobs would be inappropriate for the other sex. Students must be able to defend their opinions based on the actual duties of the jobs.

Films:

"Someone's in the Kitchen with Jamie," 28 minutes. Learning Corporation of America, Coronet/MTI Film and Video, 108 Wilmot Road, Deerfield, IL 60015; (708) 940-1260.

The star pitcher on the baseball team encourages his friends to sign up for Home Economics so his mom can keep her job. The boys and their "macho" coach discover it's okay for boys to cook and so on. The film is a bit overdone and predictable, but may spark discussion.

"The Secret of the Sexes," 60 minutes. Vestron Video, P.O. Box 10382, Stamford, CT 06901; (800) 523-5503.

Looks at how society "typecasts" young girls and boys often unconsciously. Originally broadcast as a NOVA segment on PBS.

"Sandra, Zella, Dee and Claire: Four Women in Science," 19 minutes. EDC/WEEA Publishing Center, 55 Chapel Street. Suite 200, Newton, MA 02160; (800) 225-3088

Dated, but does provide a look at the careers of four women: an astronomer, a veterinarian, a laser physicist, and an engineer.

Resources:

Dunphy, Gail. *Careers Don't Come in Pink or Blue.* Providence, RI: Rhode Island Dept. of Community Affairs, 1985.

Sims-Bell, Barbara. *Foodwork, Jobs in the Food Industry and How to Get Them,* Santa Barbara, CA, Advocacy Press, 1993.

Collage

PAGE 23 **Workbook 13**

Objective:

To show students how sex roles are projected by the media, and, thereby, strongly reinforce sex-role stereotyping.

Presentation Suggestions:

Before beginning this exercise, you might want to show the excellent film, "Killing Us Softly," by Cambridge Documentary Films. The film presents an in-depth look at the images of women in advertising. It shows how women are portrayed as sex symbols, unpleasant housewives, or supermoms, and how guilt is used to encourage women to buy products. Violence against women is also examined. After a discussion of the film, students may complete their collages.

The teacher should provide magazines, scissors, glue, and colored pens or crayons. Students can cut out words and pictures or draw images to make their compositions. Larger construction paper may be used.

Activities:

Ask students to bring in music/lyrics, tapes, or phonograph records of songs that are examples of sex-role stereotyping.

A motivated group could present a skit on the topic.

For a special project, a small group of students might put together and present a "radio show" or disco presentation featuring only music that flagrantly promotes sex-role stereotyping.

Follow-Up:

When the students have finished, ask them to share their collages.

Resources:

Film: "Killing Us Softly," Cambridge Documentary Films, Box 385, Cambridge, MA 02139. (617) 354-3677.

"Still Killing Us Softly." New Edition, 1987.

Both films present an in-depth look at the negative images of women in advertising.

What TV Tells You
What TV for Children Tells You

Workbook 14-15

Objective:

To help students evaluate the messages about sex-role stereotyping presented by television.

Presentation Suggestions:

These exercises should be assigned as homework over a one-week period. Discussion questions might include:

What activities were common to men?

What activities were common to women?

Does TV encourage sex-role stereotyping?

What impact does TV have on younger brothers and sisters?

How could television affect your life choices? How do you feel about that?

What specific commercials are particularly guilty of sex-role stereotyping? Ask students to rewrite the commercials to their satisfaction.

Students could also describe each character with an adjective or two: e.g., sexy, macho, dumb, violent, and the like. What can they conclude?

Activities:

Have students choose a particular television show or commercial that is guilty of sex-role stereotyping. Ask them to write a letter voicing objections to this practice and offering constructive suggestions. You might focus on the commercials directed toward young children and their toys. This gives the student a role as advocate for younger siblings.

Resources:

Addresses of major networks:

ABC, 1330 Avenue of the Americas, 14 New York, NY 10019.

ABC Entertainment President, 2040 Avenue of the Stars, Los Angeles, CA 90067

CBS, 51 West 52nd Street, New York, NY 10019.

CBS Entertainment President, 7800 Beverly Blvd., Los Angeles, CA 90036

CNN, One CNN Center, Atlanta, GA 30348. (404) 827-1500, FAX (405) 523-8517.

NBC, 30 Rockefeller Plaza, New York, NY 10020

NBC Entertainment President, 3000 W. Alameda, Burbank, CA 91523

Public Broadcasting Service, 1320 Braddock Pl., Alexandria, VA 22314

Federal Communications Commission Complaint & Investigation Office, 2025 M St. NW, Room 8210, Washington, DC 20554

Viewers for Quality Television, Box 195, Fairfax Station, VA 22039

IMPORTANT: This is the end of Chapter One in *Challenges*. The following two exercises appear only in Choices. Before continuing, read p. 30, which explains why and how the books differ at this point, and provides suggestions for dealing with those differences.

Women and Men in History

PAGE 27 **Workbook 16**

Objective:

To make students aware of women's contributions to society throughout history and of society's failure to acknowledge these contributions.

Presentation Suggestions:

After students have tried to complete the exercise on their own (and probably found it more difficult to fill in the female column), complete the exercise as a group. Some women's names you might include are:

Explorers: Osa Johnson, Amelia Earhart, Sally Ride, Sacajawea

Military Leaders: Joan of Arc, the biblical Deborah

Musical Composers: Carrie Jacobs Bond, Clara Schumann

National Leaders: Queen Elizabeth I, Catherine de Medici, Queen Victoria

Early American Colonial Leaders: Betsy Ross, Abigail Adams, Pocahontas, Dolly Madison

Recent National Leaders: Indira Ghandi, Margaret Thatcher, Queen Elizabeth II, Corozon Aquino

Infamous Villains: Ma Barker, Delilah, Mata Hari, Tokyo Rose

Athletes: Billy Jean King, "Babe" Didrikson Zaharias, Wilma Rudolph, Althea Gibson, Sonja Henje

United States Senators: Margaret Chase Smith, Nancy Kassebaum, Paula Hawkins, Barbara Mikulski

Authors: Jane Austen, George Sand, George Eliot, Charlotte Bronte, Virginia Woolf, Emily Dickinson, Louisa May Alcott, Gertrude Stein

Activities:

A guest speaker could discuss the role of women in history. Places to locate speakers are local college history departments, high school history departments, or women's centers.

Students could read the newspaper to discover what notable women today are doing. Who are the top ten women in today's world, in the opinion of the class?

Show the film, "One Fine Day," which is a celebration of the American woman from the 18th century to the present.

Follow-Up:

For extra credit, write an essay about an important woman in history. Include why she is important to remember, what her accomplishments were, how she came to achieve success, and what obstacles she had to overcome.

Resources:

Vare, Ethlie Ann and Greg Ptacek. *Mothers of Invention: From the Bra to the Bomb, Forgotten Women and Their Unforgettable Ideas*. New York: Quill William Morrow, 1987.

O'Neill, Lois Decker, ed. *The Women's Book of World Records and Achievements.* Information House Books, 1979.

McCullogh, Joan. *First of All-Significant "Firsts" by American Women.* New York: Holt, Rinehart, and Winston, 1980.

Films:

"One Fine Day," Ishtar Films, Box 51, Route 311, Patterson, NY 12563. (914) 878-3561 or Ishtar Films, 6253 Hollywood Blvd., Suite 623, Hollywood, CA 90028. (213) 461-1560.

"She's Nobody's Baby," NM Teleprograms, 108 Wilmot Road, Deerfield, IL 60015. (800) 323-5343. Narrated by Alan Alda and Marlo Thomas, this documentary examines women's changing roles in the twentieth century.

Broverman Scale

PAGES 28-33 **Workbook 17-18**

Objective:

To point out to students that in our society masculine characteristics may be valued more highly than feminine characteristics. This scale is an evaluation tool to begin focusing on important behavioral patterns that may limit career aspirations.

Presentation Suggestions:

Give as little direction as possible. Ask students to give first-reaction responses and to complete the first page before going to the next page.

With some groups it is necessary to explain carefully the meaning of the different characteristics before doing the exercise.

When the exercise is completed, assign numerical values to the lines as indicated on p. 31. Usually, the group average comes very close to the findings of the Broverman study. Ask the students why they think the typical male's characteristics match those perceived as "healthy" for an adult.

Activities:

Also included is an extra copy of the test to give to a friend or family member for a homework assignment. Discussion could follow.

Follow-Up:

The individual scale offers an opportunity to examine one's own characteristics in relation to those of a "Healthy Adult." On p. 113 of the text, the students are asked to return to the scale to write goals and objectives that will help them make these changes.

Resources:

Broverman, Inge K., Donald M. Broverman, Frank E. Clarkson, Paul S. Rosenkrantz, and Susan R. Vogel, "Sex-Role Stereotypes and Clinical Judgments of Mental Health," *Journal of Consulting and Clinical Psychology,* 34, no. 1 (1970): pp. 1-7.

Presentation Suggestions for the Differences between

Choices and *Challenges*

For pp. 28-43 in *Choices* and pp. 28-43 *Challenges*, we suggest assigning the exercises either in class or as homework. When completed, discuss each exercise in class as a whole group. It is important for members of both sexes to be aware of the issues covered in both *Choices* and *Challenges*. When your students realize the challenges facing them and recognize they have more choices in life, they will have a better understanding of the societal messages given to each sex and the barriers we create for ourselves.

If you are conducting either an all-male or all-female class, we suggest getting a copy of the other text to read so if any of these issues come up in discussion, you will have some ideas on how to approach them.

Chapter Two

The central issues raised in this chapter involve awakening girls to the realities of the adult world in terms of work expectations. We want them to realize that they will spend most of their lives working and that they should be paid fairly for it. Historically, women have been reluctant to say that they are working to make a lot of money. Somehow that has not been "ladylike." So they say they are working "to help people," or because they "like to be around people," or because they want to be "creative." Those are also good reasons to work, and no doubt they are true. Yet, women's disavowal of money may have an effect on the aspirations of the younger generation. The terms "power" and "money" may raise feelings of ambivalence. Financial considerations *are* important in your students' future plans. We focus on economic realities in stressing the salary differential between traditional men's jobs and traditional women's jobs. (We also recommend heightening awareness with the exercises in *Choices,* "Women and Men in History" and "What Qualities Does a Woman Possess?" at the end of Chapter One.)

We ask the boys to examine the stereotyped male, or macho role and note the effect this role can have on health and happiness. We would like them to be aware that there are choices in roles and lifestyles. The exercises in this chapter focus on quality of life. We ask the boys to think about what "being a man" means to them; to consider what advantages learning to express their feelings might have for their well-being; and to examine a balanced lifestyle. These concepts may be new to a teenage boy, but research has shown that they are important in learning to be a well-rounded individual. Also, with the economic changes that have brought women into the workforce, our young men must undergo an awakening to prepare them for the realities they will face. Most of them will *not* be the sole provider for a family, and they need to understand what a partnership will mean to them.

The Working World

PAGES 37-39 **No Workbook Page**

Objective:

To encourage students to broaden their horizons by showing the salary differential between traditionally male and female jobs.

Presentation Suggestions:

This exercise will demonstrate that traditionally male jobs certainly pay more than traditionally female jobs. Students may have a vague idea that "women's jobs" pay less than "men's jobs," but this graphic display of the inequality always comes as a jolt. It is a very effective way to encourage girls to broaden their horizons, something that should be stressed throughout the course.

Begin by discussing each job briefly, outlining the basic duties or responsibilities it entails, or ask students what they think each job involves. As a group, identify each job as traditionally male or female, based solely on the actual numbers of people working in these jobs today. Then complete the graph as directed. If only one color is used, be sure to plot the traditionally male jobs and connect the dots, and then do the same for the traditionally female jobs.

Activities:

Talk about the value of money. Do men and women feel differently about it?

You may want to talk about historical reasons for the earnings gap between the sexes. Until recently, very few girls received an education. The first coed college began admitting women less than 150 years ago. Only now, in the last ten years, are women being admitted to professional schools in meaningful numbers. Because women have had primary responsibility for housework and child care, they have not had the freedom to pursue demanding careers. In these and other ways, society has been able to channel working women into just a few "acceptable" jobs. Then, because women were supposed to be married, lower pay was justified on the basis that, while men had to support a family, women worked only for "mad money."

If students raise cries of, "It's not fair" (they probably will and they certainly should!), you can talk about the existing laws that are attempting to rectify the situation. There has been a federal law against sex discrimination in employment since 1964. That means that a woman cannot be turned down for a job just because she is a woman, and that men and women should be paid the same for doing the same job. Unfortunately, the law is not rigidly enforced and employers have found many ways to circumvent it.

Follow-Up:

Refer to the issue of money and nontraditional and careers often throughout the course.

Resources:

Occupational Outlook Handbook, U.S. Department of Labor, Bureau of Labor Statistics.*

Monthly Labor Review, U.S. Department of Labor, Bureau of Labor Statistics.*

Occupational Outlook Quarterly, U.S. Department of Labor, Bureau of Labor Statistics.*

Kosterlitz, Julie, and Florence Graves. "Should Nurses Be Paid as Much as Truck Drivers?" Debate between Betty Friedan and Phyllis Schlafly. *Common Cause,* March/April 1983.

Ricci, Larry J. *High Paying Blue-Collar Jobs for Women.* New York: Ballantine Books, 1981.

Wright, John W. *The American Almanac of Jobs and Salaries,* revised ed. New York: Avon Books, 1987.

* Available in libraries.

Women in the Workforce

PAGES 41-42 **Workbook 21**

Objective:

To make students aware of facts about employment for women and men.

Presentation Suggestions:

After the students have taken this quiz, discuss the answers in detail. Both boys and girls can benefit from the knowledge, and most are surprised at what they learn. The class leader should refer back to these statistics throughout the course.

Resources:

Andrews, Lori B. "Myths and Facts about Working Women." *Parents Magazine,* 58, July 1983, p. 26.

"20 Facts on Women Workers," U.S. Department of Labor, Office of the Secretary, Women's Bureau, 1986.

Today's Girls-Tomorrow's Women. (A National Seminar, June 13-15, 1978, Wingspread Conference Center, Racine, Wisconsin), reprinted, Girls Incorporated, 1980. Contact the National Girls Incorporated Resource Center, 441 West Michigan St., Indianapolis, IN 46202

Lenz, Elinor, and Barbara Myerhoss. *The Feminization of America.* Los Angeles, CA: Jeremy P. Tarcher, 1985.

Wright, Barbara Drygulski, ed. *Women, Work and Technology.* Ann Arbor: The University of Michigan Press, 1990.

Learning to Be a Man

PAGE 29 **Workbook 22**

Objective:

To have students rate themselves using a chart of traditionally "male" characteristics. Through discussion, find out where and how these attitudes were developed and what impact they have on the quality of life (satisfaction in relationships and employment, impact on health and life span).

Presentation Suggestions:

Assign pp. 28-29. Discussion for this exercise and "What Qualities Does a Woman Possess?" in *Choices* should complement each other.

Activities:

Brainstorm words associated with the "traditionally masculine role." Examples: tough, cool, macho, hero, aggressive, stoic, knight in shining armor, strong, unchangeable, provider, hunter, unfeeling, fearless, unemotional, independent, controlled, predictable, winner, powerful, successful, and the like.

Then ask students to think of some situations in which these characteristics could be helpful to them as individuals, and some situations in which they could be harmful.

Resources:

Goldberg, Herb. *The Hazards of Being Male*. New York: The New American Library, 1976.

Goldberg, Herb. *The New Male*. New York: The New American Library, 1979.

Films:

"Another Half," 27 minutes. Bill Wadsworth Productions, 1913 W. 37th St., Austin, TX 78731; (512) 478-2971.

An award-winning video about two boys and their struggle to broaden the boundaries of their masculinity. It will stimulate discussion among both males and females concerning gender-role pressures, sex-role stereotyping, sexual responsibility and life planning.

"Heroes and Strangers," 29 minutes. New Day Films, 121 W. 27th St., Suite 202, New York, NY 10001; (212) 645-8210.

Reveals the attitudes and customs which limit men's involvement in families. Raises questions about work and gender roles.

"New Relations-A Film about Fathers and Sons," 34 minutes. Fanlight Productions, 47 Halifax Street, Boston, MA 02130; (617) 524-0980.

Explores a couple's choice to share child care as well as the costs and rewards of having children late in life.

Hazards of "Being a Man"

PAGES 30-31 **Workbook 22-23**

Objective:

To help students visualize the health statistics for stress-related problems in men and women. This will stimulate discussion on the "costs" of the traditionally masculine role.

Presentation Suggestions:

Ask students to complete this chart on their own. It is an ideal time to assign the "Working World" exercise in *Choices* to the girls (p. 37). Once these exercises are completed, ask the young women to report on their findings and the young men to report on theirs. When these exercises and charts are compared, some students may be concerned that the "costs" of the male lifestyle are too high. The young women may think that if they choose a traditionally male job paying a higher salary, these stress responses will be the price, and that they are unwilling to pay that price. This concern needs to be addressed before the course continues. Motivating young women to look seriously at traditionally male careers as a choice for them is one of the main goals of this curriculum.

How do you as an instructor respond?

Some examples: The chart of the differences in health statistics may reflect the lifestyle men have adopted. Many men feel that in order to be a man they must act tough, cool and controlled. Stress can come from the way in which men approach a job, and is not necessarily inherent in the job itself Sometimes, or instance, accidents occur because the person thought he could "tough out" a situation or did not take precautions.

Many women entering the workforce in nontraditional jobs have adopted this tough, cool, controlled mode of operation to try to fit in. When this happens, they too experience stress.

In general, people who are satisfied with their work and can put their lives in reasonable perspective are less likely to suffer from stress, no matter what the job.

Activities:

Start the class off with the question, 'What is the most important asset we have as individuals?" Note that if an older person is asked this question, the answer will likely be "health." Teens may have trouble seeing this, so you might discuss the subject. Then ask, "Why do you think men have more health problems related to stress than women?" Answers will probably include "working harder," "more responsibility," "feeling locked in," and "more dangerous careers."

Brainstorm how they as individuals can live a lifestyle that will *not* be hazardous to their health and well-being. What are the elements of a healthy lifestyle? (A balanced lifestyle will be discussed on pp. 40-42 in *Challenges.*)

Resources:

Friggens, Paul. "The Indispensable Man Is Only a Modern Myth." *Nation's Business,* 67, May 1979, p. 63.

Expressing Emotion

PAGES 32-33 **Workbook 24**

Objective:

To have young men reflect on the messages society has given them about expressing emotion (sadness, hurt, frustration, fear, affection, and the like) and to encourage them to examine the message that expressing these emotions is not masculine.

Presentation Suggestions:

Ask students to read the story and fill out the questionnaire. Then as a class discuss the answers.

Males are typically conditioned to believe that the word "emotional" is synonymous with "feminine." This is tragic, since it places severe limitations on their capacity for growth. It is important that males learn to think of their emotions as feelings to be recognized and dealt with rather than as feelings to be controlled or denied.

Feelings may be a difficult subject for some students to discuss in a group. If you sense this, divide the class into pairs for discussion purposes. If any student has suffered a recent loss, be particularly sensitive to his/her needs.

Activities:

Read a list of situations that evoke emotions in men and women. Ask the class how a "typical" woman and a "typical" man would respond. What might they feel and how might they express their feelings?

Suggestions:

1. You have asked, or been asked, for a date to a school dance. After much anticipation, expense (new clothes) and special arrangements, you are ready. Your date does not arrive and you find that she/he has gone to a movie.

2. You have just been told your parents are getting a divorce and you will be moving out of the state in two weeks.

3. The local radio station is having a statewide contest. You and all your friends have entered. The station has just announced that you won a new car!

As students discuss these or other situations, encourage them to think of different ways in which feelings can be expressed. Introduce the concept that the first step in being genuine is recognizing what you feel. The second step is in saying what that feeling is: "I feel angry," "I'm really happy," "I'm frustrated," and so on.

Resources:

Naifek, Steven, and Gregory White Smith. *Why Can't Men Open Up?* New York: Clarkson N. Potter, 1984.

The Meaning of Success

PAGES 34-35 **Workbook 25**

Objective:

To have students examine the many areas in their lives where they can be "successful." Also to help them develop their own definition of success rather than accept the one presented by the media.

Presentation Suggestions:

Before reading the exercise, ask the class, "When I say the word 'success,' what word do you think of?" Most of the students, particularly the males, will answer in financial terms.

Discuss the quotations on p. 34. What terms do those quoted equate with success (contentment, individuality, relationships, effort, ethical behavior, self-knowledge, e.g.)?

Activities:

Discuss the word "failure." Ask the students to think about a perceived failure in their lives and to share any positive consequences resulting from that experience. It is hoped the students will share *growth* experiences. You may ask them to share this exercise with a parent.

Ask the students the question, "What is the fear of failure, and how does this limit our lives?"

Work: The Love/Hate Relationship

PAGES 36-37 **No Workbook Page**

Objective:

To have the students recognize the need to plan carefully for their futures.

Presentation Suggestions:

Discuss the quotations on p. 36. You may want to ask the students to choose the quotation they most readily relate to and to discuss that quotation in a small group. How common do they think these feelings are? Can one person relate to all of them?

Activities:

Do any students know an adult who does not like the work he/she does? Have those students ask three adults why they continue to work at that job. The answer will probably be feelings of "responsibility" or of being "locked in." Discuss how careful planning now can help students avoid this unhappy fate.

The New Partnerships

PAGES 38-39 **No Workbook Page**

Objective:

To show young men that the economic emergence of women in society can benefit men as well as women.

Presentation Suggestions:

Discuss some of the benefits that might come from a marriage in which both partners have the capability to pursue careers that pay decent, livable wages.

Activities:

Ask students to share stories similar to Tom's and Cindy's that they may have seen or heard about from their own families and acquaint acquaintances.

Resources:

Bingham, Mindy and Sandy Stryker. *More Choices: A Strategic Planning Guide for Mixing Career and Family*. Santa Barbara: Advocacy Press, 1987, pp. 155-171.

Balancing Your Life

PAGES 40-42 **Workbook 26-27**

Objective:

To examine what constitutes a balanced lifestyle and visually analyze what is balanced and what is unbalanced, so the students can evaluate their own lives in future years.

Presentation Suggestions:

Discuss the definitions of the three areas of life (see text). Ask students to give examples of what activities might fall in each area.

Activities:

Have students complete the exercises in the book, either in a discussion group or on their own. Assign p. 42 in *Challenges* as homework and then discuss the examples the next day.

Poll the class on the responses received from the men over 30. If lifestyles were out of balance, in which area (wedge) were men most likely to be spending too much time? The response will probably be "career." Discuss what the cost of this action might be in the long run.

Chapter Three

Chapter Three is a critical one. Dealing with the high cost of living can be depressing and it's important to be enthusiastic as you bring your students through this lengthy exercise. If you can get excited about this topic, your students will, too. Though young people often don't have the slightest idea what things cost, they are interested. As they near the age of independence, they see the relevance in these figures.

What they often *can't* see is how their career choice will affect their economic well-being. How can we talk about choosing a career if students don't know how much it will cost to live the life they would like to have? For women particularly, understanding this relationship is critical. Just as they don't know very much about what things cost, they don't realize how much they might expect to earn at different jobs, or what a disparity there is in salary ranges.

The main part of this chapter involves actually setting up a budget. You will need to be a resource person for your students, bringing in newspapers, a calculator or two, perhaps your own utility bills or grocery tapes. Students may need scissors and tape or glue, or they may copy ads in their books. You may have to help students individually with some of the more involved processes, such as the section on financing a home. In some cases, you may end up doing all the math. That's okay. The goal is to illustrate how much things cost.

When the budget is completed, we ask students to find a job that could support them, according to their budget. Again, you will need to provide want ads, perhaps from a publication such as the *Wall Street Journal,* as well as from local or regional newspapers. At this point, many students begin to change their minds about their future careers. This chapter demonstrates to them the importance of thinking about money when they make career choices.

The section called "True Stories" shows that not being able to support oneself is a risky way to live, as may be having one person solely responsible for the financial stability of a family.

Interesting Note: In evaluation after evaluation, students have identified the budget exercise as their favorite exercise.

Interview

PAGES 47-48 **Workbook 28-29**

Objective:

To point out to students that young men are usually more self-directed and career-conscious than young women.

Presentation Suggestions:

Ask the students to interview their peers, three young men and three young women. Students may be able to set up an interview table in the cafeteria or to pass out interview questions in one of their classes.

Follow-Up:

From their small sample, students may not immediately leap to the conclusion that young men have given their futures more thought than young women. To help them reach this point, lead them ahead by short steps. Compile statistics for the whole class on the board. Then discuss:

1. How many of the young men had a definite career goal?
2. How many of the young women had a definite career goal?
3. Of the young women who had a definite career goal, how many had chosen a traditionally female career?
4. How many young women had chosen a job that, on average, pays more than $15,000 a year?

Statistics show that of jobs paying over $15,000 a year, 90 percent are held by men. While eight-tenths of 1 percent of working women make over $25,000 per year, 12 percent of the working men do.

True Stories

PAGES 49-54 **Workbook 30-34**

Objective:

To make students aware of unexpected events that actually do happen in life. Some things cannot be controlled or predicted. In *Choices,* the problem encountered would be easier to handle if women were better prepared economically. *Challenges* considers the same stories from the male viewpoint.

Presentation Suggestions:

Read the stories aloud and discuss them, or ask students to read the stories and answer the questions that follow each of them. For special populations the teacher may record these stories on audio tape, so the student may listen to them individually. If your class is large, you might break into groups, with each group discussing one story and then reporting back to the class.

Activities:

Invite a panel of women who have survived economic crises to discuss how they handled them and how they might have been better prepared, if they were not prepared.

_______________ 's Story

PAGE 55 **Workbook 35**

Objective:

To personalize the "True Stories," and bring the students' awareness closer to home.

Presentation Suggestions:

Upon completing the "True Stories" exercise, ask students to think of an acquaintance who has been faced with a similar economic crisis. Almost all students will know someone about whom they can write. Ask them to interview that person if they can.

Budget

PAGES 56-81 Workbook 36-47

Objective:

To help students realize how much income they will need to live as they would like at age 28, and to show that in order to achieve that income, career preparedness should begin in their teens.

Presentation Suggestions:

Ask your students to fantasize. What kind of life will they have when they are 28? (30 is too old for them to relate to!) Will they own a home? What kind of car will they drive? Will they take vacations? Where would they like to go? Take out your "magic wand," tap it, and say, "Okay. You *are* 28. You have the family and the life you're thinking about. There's just one catch. You are the sole provider for yourself and your children. We want you to figure out the bottom line costs for supporting yourself and your children."

In class, working through a typical example on the board helps demonstrate the procedures. First, the class needs to decide the number of children and pets for their "typical" person.

Example:

28 years old

5-year-old boy

3-year-old girl

dog

In order to complete their individual budgets, students look back at the exercise, "Envision Your Life." If they expected to have children in that exercise, they now have those children. It's up to them to choose the ages and sexes of the "family." Also ask if students expect to have pets. If so, they need to list the pets along with their family. (Pets become a crucial factor when choosing a place to rent.)

One word of caution: Encourage students to be realistic. Most students will have a tendency to dream of lifestyles seen on their favorite television shows. If the necessary income is *too* high, some students might give up before they begin. Gauge your examples to reflect the middle income level of your students. When someone in class wants a Porsche and the rest of the class nods in approval, include a less expensive alternative, as well.

If the entire budget exercise is to be completed in a short time period, i.e., one to two hours, the group example is all you'll have time for. Have the class vote on the makeup of its' "family."

Housing:

To find acceptable housing, give students the classified ad sections from a local newspaper, and ask them to find the cost of renting and buying a place to live. Then compare the two options. Besides cost, consider size, location, suitability for children or pets, and extras (pool, exercise room, garage, yard). Discuss the advantages and disadvantages of renting and buying. For example, renting might be cheaper. It allows the occupant to be more mobile. Apartments often have pools, exercise rooms, and other luxuries a young homeowner may not be able to afford. But apartments may not allow children or pets. Rent can be raised.

The occupant isn't gaining equity. Buying on the other hand, gives the owners the freedom to do almost whatever they like with the property. Homeowners know in advance what their payments are going to be. There are tax advantages. There is pride in ownership. However, homes also require maintenance. Down payments are quite large. People who own their homes are less free to pick up and move.

Utilities:

After students have figured their monthly payments, they often assume their housing costs are taken care of. You might ask them to consider what they get for their monthly housing (floors, walls, and so on). Point out that if they'd like lights, water, gas for the stove and so on, they will have to make additional payments. Most students have no idea what gas or electricity costs. Have them bring utility bills from home, bring in your own, or get the average cost from utility companies. Don't forget to include such utilities as cable TV and long-distance phone calls. Try to draw students out as you go through the budget. They need to make definite decisions.

Transportation:

This is one area in which students let their imaginations run wild. Again, you will need to furnish the classified ad section of the local paper. Will students want a new car, or will a used vehicle serve the purpose? Registration and insurance costs vary widely throughout the country. You may need to call an insurance agent to get an estimate of rates for a 28-year-old. Again, you may have to help some students with the math.

Clothing:

The cost of clothing is one topic with which young people are acquainted. Since they are likely to spend all of their disposable income for clothes, it may be almost impossible to get them to be realistic. But remind students that they are not starting from scratch. They only need to replace certain items in their wardrobe. Remind them, too, that their career choice will dictate to some extent what kind of clothes they will need. Right now, they may be able to get by with a dozen pair of blue jeans, but some careers require more formal dress. Others require uniforms. Many of the girls in class will want to be actresses or dancers. Remind them of the cost of audition clothes.

Food:

You and/or your students can bring in grocery tapes. This is a good consumer education chapter. Perhaps you could have a home economics teacher or home extension agent address the class about keeping food costs down. Ask each student to interview parents on what their average weekly grocery bill is.

Entertainment:

This is a topic that gives students a chance to dream. Entertainment often is curtailed when funds are tight, though most people really dislike cutting it. If students say they can get along without entertainment or vacations, remind them that for fifty weeks of the year, they will be working full-time, trying to take care of their children, keeping house, and so on. They probably will rise at 6 a.m. and collapse exhausted at 10 p.m., without time to do anything for themselves. Parents need and deserve a vacation, too. Allow the students who really like to dream to dream. This could make the difference between deciding to become an accountant instead of a bookkeeper.

Health Care:

Discussion of this topic will probably take the form of "what it is" rather than whether it's needed or how much it costs. Stress the fact that one benefit of having a full-time job is that the employer usually pays all or most of the cost of health insurance. Dental insurance is another frequent benefit. Without health insurance, a serious illness or accident could easily bankrupt a family. Most part-time jobs do not include medical insurance as a benefit.

Child Care:

Child care is an essential, yet expensive, budgetary item for most working parents. Perhaps you could assign students to check the cost of various sorts of child care (day-care centers, day-care homes, live-in housekeepers, and the like). These figures will come in handy in discussions in Chapter Seven. Child-care figures should be adapted to the number and ages of children in the fictional family.

Savings:

Students are likely to inquire why, at age 28, they need to be saving. Some of the reasons you'll want to discuss include major household or auto repairs, the possibility of unemployment, college tuition for the children, major purchases such as a down payment for a house, vacations and retirement. Perhaps you could have a couple visit the class to discuss how they're planning for retirement, or schedule as a guest speaker someone who's living solely on Social Security.

Miscellaneous:

Besides toys, gifts, and pets, ask students to consider charitable contributions or contributions to a church.

We've found that the budget section generates enthusiasm in class. Students have their own ideas and values and want to share them. By the end of the exercise, they're interested in looking for a job that pays enough to live on.

Activities:

Create a personal budget based on the money each student now receives from an allowance or a part-time job.

Compare classified employment ads from newspapers in different parts of the country. Public libraries usually have many newspapers. Discuss the differences noted.

Discuss consumer education. How can costs of food, clothing, and the like, be reduced?

What are the advantages of buying a house as opposed to renting one?

How is energy conservation important in keeping costs low?

What does "A penny saved is a penny earned" mean? Actually, because of the tax structure of this country, it should be, "A penny saved is $.0125 earned." Why?

Bring in a speaker to discuss buying on credit. Usually, banks can provide assistance in this area.

Some students think that welfare payments will cover their needs. They have seen several generations of their family survive on welfare and do not know how small the payments really are. In that case, work through a budget using the amount of *expected* welfare payments as the total income. As they try to make up a suitable budget, students will see that welfare payments are not sufficient to provide them with a comfortable lifestyle. After this, do the budget exercise once more with this group as previously outlined.

Follow-Up:

Ask students to share their budget with their parents. This could stimulate important discussions between parent and student about economic considerations that have never been openly discussed.

Film:

Video: "Gentle Angry People," Catholic Charities USA, 1319 F Street N.W., Washington D.C., 20004. (202) 639-8400.

Using interviews and real-life situations, the effects of poverty amidst middle-aged and older rural Americans is discussed.

Now Find a Job

PAGE 84 **Workbook 47**

Objective:

To help students see the connection between economic preparedness and the career-planning process.

Presentation Suggestions:

When students' gross monthly requirement has been determined, the instructor should circulate classified sections of newspapers (local and big city). Ask students to find a job that they will be qualified for that will adequately support them and their family at age 28 in the lifestyle they described. At this point, students can really see how their career choices will affect the way they live.

Activities:

Visit a library or career center to research employment salary levels.

Invite an employment counselor or personnel director of a large company to talk with students about salaries and how they are set.

Ask students to look back at the "Envision Your Life" exercise. Would their proposed activity at age 28 support their lifestyle?

If your students live in an economically depressed area, be sure to get newspapers from other areas of the state or country. Hold a discussion on the advantages and disadvantages of moving from your hometown to a diffrent city or state.

Follow-Up:

You now have the students' attention. They should become much more personally involved in the career-planning process. Refer to the results of this exercise often as you work through the book.

Resources:

Occupational Outlook Handbook, U.S. Department of Labor, Bureau of Labor Statistics. Available in libraries.

Occupational Outlook Quarterly, U.S. Department of Labor, Bureau of Labor Statistics. Available in libraries.

Monthly Labor Review, U.S. Department of Labor, Bureau of Labor Statistics. Available in libraries.

Skolnick, Joan, Carol Langbort and Lucille Day. *How to Encourage Girls in Math and Science: Strategies for Parents and Educators.* Palo Alto: Dale Seymour Publications, 1982.

Ricci, Larry J. *High-Paying Blue-Collar Jobs for Women.* New York: Ballantine Books, 1981.

Wright, John W. *The American Almanac of Jobs and Salaries,* revised ed. New York: Avon Books, 1987.

CHAPTER FOUR

Knowing What You Want Out of Life

Values clarification and goal setting

Whenever two good people argue over principles, they are both right
— Marie Ebner von Eschenbach
Austrian Author

You have to know exactly what you want out of your career. If you want to be a star, you don't bother with other things.
— Marilyn Horne
Opera Singer

87

CHAPTER FOUR

Knowing What You Want Out of Life

Values clarification and goal setting

There is no duty we so much underrate as the duty of being happy
— Robert Louis Stevenson
Author

87

Chapter Four

We've found the self-discovery chapters to be especially popular with students. This chapter combines values clarification, one of the best-received sections of the book, with goal setting, which can be a little more difficult to teach. Both parts are extremely important and, in combination, can start students thinking about careers they haven't considered before. For example, one 14-year-old told us that having scored high in the money and power categories, she is now seriously working toward the goal of becoming an international stockbroker.

Remind students that, as they complete the values survey, they need to be honest with themselves. The survey is not designed to measure the values of their parents or their friends. Unless they honestly assess their own feelings, the exercise will be useless. Another important discussion topic is the temporary nature of the importance of some values and the need to reassess values throughout life.

Goal setting is a more difficult concept for students. Have they ever made New Year's resolutions? Aren't they goals? Why not set goals for each week or each month? For motivation, students can reward themselves every time they meet a goal: perhaps a movie or hot fudge sundae for meeting a small goal, new clothes or a day trip for larger or long-term goals.

To impress students with the roles values clarification and goal setting will play throughout their lives, ask them to take a look at the last chapter of this book. These exercises are not to be completed until the students are older. Values and goals come into play when considering whether or whom to marry ("Should I Marry This Man/Woman?"), how to raise children ("Now That I'm a Mother/Father"), planning for the unforeseen ("An Exercise for Everyone"), reevaluating career plans ("Should I Change Careers?"), and having a rewarding life in later years ("Filling the Gaps"). Acquiring this knowledge now will give students a head start toward a satisfying future.

What Do I Enjoy Doing?

PAGES 90-91 **Workbook 48**

Objective:

To show students the relationship between what they enjoy and what is important to them at this time.

Presentation Suggestions:

This exercise should help students make generalizations about their interests and activities. Ask them to look for patterns such as, "I like to do things mainly with people," "Most things I like to do cost money," or "I like to be physically active." Think of additional categories. For example, "Does this activity require a physical or emotional risk"?

Activities:

Have students make a personal collage by cutting out pictures or words from magazines showing how they see themselves today. For example, those students who enjoy the outdoors might include pictures of hiking and camping; students who enjoy cars might display pictures of racing or car shows.

Follow-Up:

Suggest that students repeat this exercise in two years. Emphasize the fact that students will have many new experiences in their late teen years, and they may greatly enjoy some activities they haven't even thought about yet. Noting what they enjoy most about an activity can help students choose a career.

Values Survey

PAGES 93-97 **Workbook 49-53**

Objective:

To have students discern some of the values most important to them.

Presentation Suggestions:

Emphasize the importance of answering each question on the basis of how the *students feel,* not how they *think they should* answer. After students have completed and scored their own values survey, remind them to be aware that personal values change with time and circumstances. Therefore, encourage them to reexamine their values every few years.

To avoid having to turn pages back and forth frequently while scoring the survey, Alice Halberstadt, a teacher for learning-handicapped junior high students in California, suggests the following: After the survey is completed, furnish each student an answer sheet numbered to 104. After each number, have the student place his/her score for that statement. The student then transfers the information from the answer sheet to the survey summary in the book.

Activities:

Give each student an imaginary $1,000 an ask him/her to discuss orally, or put into writing, how she/he would spend the money.

Follow-Up:

Discuss the definitions of each value category on pp. 98-100. Students need to have a clear idea of what each value title represents, and how it relates to career choice.

Resources:

Simon, Sidney B., Leland W. Howe, and Howard Kirschenbaum. *Values Clarification: A Handbook for Teachers and Students,* revised ed. New York: A and W Publishers, Inc., 1972.

Quiz: Applying Value Categories

PAGES 101-102 **Workbook 54**

Objective:

To help students relate abstract values to specific careers. It should also help students understand the importance of choosing a career consistent with their values.

Presentation Suggestions:

After discussing the meaning of each value, ask the students to complete the quiz on p. 101. Answers are given on p. 102.

Activities:

Ask the class to think of careers that would be appropriate for each value category.

Examples:

Family: teacher, school counselor, day-care worker, librarian, home extension agent, free-lance writer, plumber.

Adventure: diplomat, tour guide, pilot, military officer, astronaut, oil rig worker, travel agent.

Knowledge: professor, librarian, journalist, historian, scientist, researcher, information officer.

Power: politician, business executive, lobbyist, school principal, member of the clergy, union official, contractor, head chef.

Moral judgment and personal consistency: environmentalist, social worker, political analyst, member of the clergy, psychologist.

Money: banker, lawyer, doctor, dentist, business executive, stockbroker, entertainer, author, real estate agent.

Friendship and companionship: public relations executive, advertising executive, salesperson, tour guide, office worker, hairdresser.

Recognition: politician, actor, writer, musician, doctor, professional athlete, horse trainer.

Independence and freedom: entrepreneur, forest ranger, salesperson, free-lancer, repair person, artist, wallpaper hanger.

Security: accountant, corporate officer, manager, government employee, maintenance person, auto mechanic, court reporter, pharmacist, optometrist, computer programmer.

Beauty or aesthetics: interior designer, gallery operator, fashion designer, buyer for department store, potter, jeweler, artist.

Creativity: writer, architect, chef, photographer, design engineer, furniture builder, program developer for a youth agency.

Helping others: police officer, fire fighter, psychiatrist, lawyer, surgeon, philanthropist, teacher.

Careers/Values

PAGE 104 **Workbook 55**

Objective:

To personalize the messages of the previous values exercises.

Presentation Suggestions:

Split the class into groups of three or four students each. Ask students to share their top three values from the values survey with others in the group. Ask the group to come up with career ideas to fit each cluster of values.

Reunite the class so students may share their ideas.

Examples:

Values	Careers
Security, knowledge, recognition	College professor, corporate manager, school principal, doctor, TV camera operator.
Money, power, creativity	Stockbroker, film producer, magazine editor, lawyer, politician, contractor.
Family, knowledge, friendship	Teacher, librarian, researcher, dietitian, counselor, computer salesperson, construction worker.
Adventure, knowledge, friendship	Detective, archaeologist, research scientist, appraiser, environmentalist, small business owner, rancher.
Moral judgment, beauty, independence	Forest ranger, philanthropist, film maker, art director, author.

Activities:

Ask a professional who has changed careers to speak about that change and what prompted it. Ask what was the most difficult aspect in making this change? What was the most exciting aspect? Then ask if the change has been a happy one. Listen for how a change in values may have been a contributing factor in deciding to change careers.

Follow-Up:

As an ongoing exercise, whenever a specific career is mentioned during class, have students consider what values would be appropriate for someone holding that job.

What Is Most Important to Me

PAGE 105 **Workbook 56**

Objective:

To encourage students to synthesize all they have learned about themselves from this chapter.

Presentation Suggestions:

Talk about how values change over the course of a person's life. For example, someone just out of school might value adventure highly. That same person, newly married, might value security. When the family of our fictional person is grown, companionship might be the top value. After retirement, that person might once again be seeking adventure. Suggest that students continue to ask themselves one question throughout their lives: "What is most important to me right now?"

Set Your Own Goals

PAGES 108-109 Workbook 57

Objective:

To give students practice in setting goals.

Presentation Suggestions:

We have found that learning to set goals and determine action steps (objectives) is difficult for many teens. Generalizations and fantasies abound. For example, students will say, "I'm going to be rich." When asked how they plan to become rich, however, they answer, "I don't know. I just will." The same is often true of feelings toward marriage. They say they will have a perfect marriage without any idea of how to achieve this idealistic state other than finding someone who will "truly love me enough."

Discuss goals in class before assigning this exercise. Some possible goals:

Today

Complete math assignment.
Practice flute for one hour.
Take books back to the library.
Call friend about weekend plans.

This Week

Finish reading novel for book report.
Send invitations for party.
Clean closet.
Take sweaters to cleaner.

This Year

Get an A in biology.
Talk with counselor about next year's classes.
Research five careers in math or science.
Take a dance class.

By Age 25

Graduate from college.
Earn $20,000 a year.
Buy a home.
Travel to Europe.

Objectives

PAGES 110-111 **Workbook 58**

Objective:

To have students learn to write specific objectives which, when put together, make up a step-by-step action plan toward completing a goal.

Presentation Suggestions:

We have found that diagramming a statement helps students see if their objective has all three components:

What will be different?

By how many?

By when?

Practice as a group before asking students to do these exercises on their own. Other goals that students may be able to develop objectives for are:

To be accepted at the state university after high school graduation.

1. To write for the catalog and entrance requirements during sophomore year of high school.
2. To take the college entrance exam during junior year.
3. To earn at least a B average during junior and senior years of high school.
4. To send in an application by the deadline.

To make the high school basketball team next year.

1. To practice after school every day this year.
2. To go to basketball camp this summer.
3. To play on an intramural team this winter.

To buy a car by the end of the year.

1. To get a job by February and save $100 per month.
2. To visit three car lots and complete research by July.
3. To begin reading used car ads in September.
4. To tell five of my parents' friends I'm looking for a clean, used car by May.
5. To read one book on auto maintenance and repair by September.

To get a date with Brent by next month.

1. To say "Hi" to Brent when I see him in the hall next Tuesday.
2. To ask Brent to dance at the party Friday night.
3. To invite Brent to a party next week.

To take a trip to Hawaii this summer.

1. To send for travel brochures by February.
2. Call a travel agent and inquire about costs.
3. To save $100 per month until next summer.
4. To make plane and hotel reservations by May 1.

Activities:

The teacher can prepare incomplete objectives and let the class state why they are incomplete.

Examples:

Go on a diet and lose 20 pounds.	By when?
Get a good education.	What will be different? By when?
Learn to play the piano.	By when?
Marry and have children before I'm 30.	How many?
Improve my typing by summer.	By how much?
Learn to cook Italian food.	By when?

Follow-Up:

It is important that students become adept at writing good, quantitative goals and objectives. This skill is used extensively throughout the text.

Film:

"Follow Your Dream," 6 1/2 minutes. 1988. YWCA Leadership Development Center, 8440 North 25th St., Phoenix, AZ 85021. (602) 944-0569.

Writing Goals and Objectives

PAGES 112-113 **Workbook 59**

Objective:

To give students more practice in writing quantitative goals and objectives.

Presentation Suggestions:

Discuss examples as a class before asking students to write their own goals and objectives. A few examples are provided below.

To make one new friend by the end of the school year.

1. To say "Hi" to three new people each school day.
2. To approach one person I don't know at every after-game dance this season.
3. To join an interest group by next month.

To avoid catching the flu this winter.

1. To eat three sensible meals a day.
2. To get eight hours of sleep each night.
3. To take a vitamin pill each morning.
4. To wear a hat and boots in wet and/or freezing weather.

To be elected to the student council next year.

1. To make myself visible by offering to chair the arrangements committee for the class dance this spring.
2. To write an agenda listing my concerns about and objectives for the school during summer vacation.
3. To nominate myself or ask a friend to nominate me when nominations are open in September.

To be admitted to medical school when I graduate from college.

1. To take as many science classes as I can in high school.
2. Interview two physicians or medical students by the end of high school.
3. To be admitted to a pre-med program during my sophomore year at college.
4. To earn at least a 3.5 grade point average over my four years of college.
5. To apply to at least three medical schools early in my senior year at college.

Activities:

Have students make two collages by cutting out words and pictures from magazines. The first collage should represent "Where I Am Now." The second should show "Where I Want to Be at Age 25." Then have students write one goal for each title. Example: By age 25 I want to have a college degree and be employed as an accountant.

Some instructors have students write goals to be completed in one month, one year, or even five years. Then they mail students their goals at the end of the time period, so they may evaluate and see how they're doing.

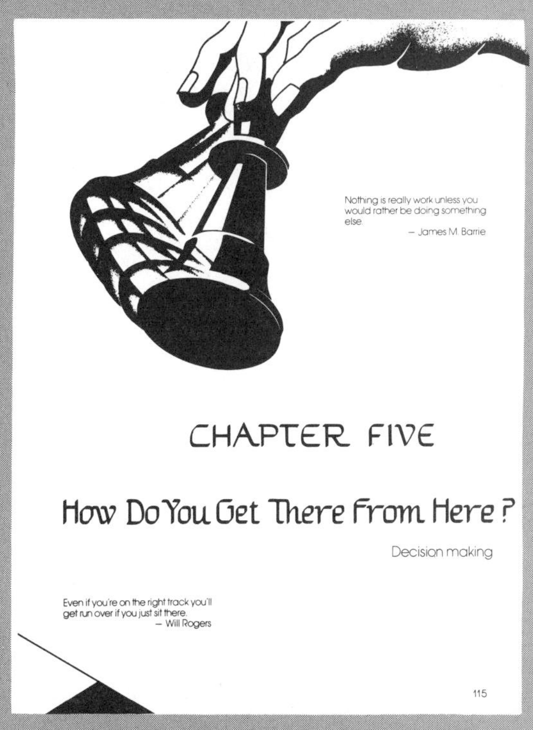

Chapter Five

Our goal in this chapter is to have students learn a basic, four-step decision-making process, which will be useful to them every time they need to make a major decision or even a small one. The first step is to state the decision to be made or the problem to be solved. It sounds easy but often we are not aware of a specific problem. We just know something is wrong or something needs to be done. For example, a person who has taken on too many activities and responsibilities may feel unsatisfied and exhausted without quite realizing why. The process of putting feelings into words helps make clear what needs to be done.

Our second step is to list alternatives. There are disadvantages as well as advantages to every alternative. Making lists of what they are also helps to clarify an issue. When followed by step three, evaluating the alternatives, we are well on our way toward making a good decision. The trick here is to find out as much about each alternative as possible through research, asking questions, or just soul-searching. Finally, we need to consider the odds. If enough information has been gathered, we can be fairly accurate in guessing the outcome of any action.

The chapter ends with a look at risk taking. Many women have been conditioned to believe that they should never do anything that causes them the slightest fear or anxiety. People don't advance very far with that philosophy. Many men have been encouraged to take great physical risks but are very uncomfortable with emotional risks. We hope that students will learn to discern between the foolish and dangerous risks, and those which, while frightening, can lead to much more satisfying lives. Perhaps you can think of a risk you took that turned out well to share with the class. Or ask class members to describe risks they've taken. What happened to them when they failed? How did they feel when they succeeded? Was it worth it?

Remind students that their decision-making skills will come in handy later in life. Refer to the "Should I Marry This Woman/Man?" and "Should I Change Careers?" exercises in Chapter Twelve.

Sandy's Story

PAGE 117 **Workbook 60**

Objective:

To help identify situations requiring decisions and point out that we are constantly making decisions, whether we realize it or not.

Presentation Suggestions:

Students have little trouble listing ten decisions to be made during a typical day. Give some examples: what time to get up, what to wear, what to have for breakfast, whether to go to class, whether to answer the teacher's questions, to study math or English first, to have lunch with friends or go to the library, to say "Hi" to Steve in the hall, to go right home after school or to have a Coke with friends, and so on. Ask students what kinds of decisions are hardest to make. Why? Which are the easiest?

Not Deciding Is Making a Decision

PAGE 119 **Workbook 61**

Objective:

To encourage students to think about the consequences of not making a decision. The passive approach often leads to undesirable results.

Presentation Suggestions:

Ask students to share with the class an instance in which they put off making a decision. What was the outcome of this procrastination? Some examples might be putting off applying for college until the admission deadline has passed, putting off homework until the night before finals, or putting off balancing your checkbook until the bank notifies you that you are overdrawn.

Decision-Making Process

PAGES 120-133 **Workbook 61-68**

Objective:

To present and have students work through a four-step decision-making model. Students will be expected to use this model throughout the book.

Presentation Suggestions:

While students can usually work through the process on their own, it is helpful to discuss responses as a group to make sure the concepts are clear. Again, try to help students be as specific as possible.

Activities:

Many students are not aware of either the number of decisions they make every day or the many alternatives available to them. Teens do have many choices. Ask students to keep a log of the decisions they make over the period of a week or a month. Were they surprised at the number? Did they think about alternatives? Do they think they made good decisions? Why or why not?

To help students practice making real-life decisions, provide an anonymous question box. Students could put questions or problems in during the week, and then the teacher could review them to screen any that would be inappropriate for class discussion. Once a week the questions or problems could be shared, and the class and the decision-making process used to develop suggestions, strategies, or action plans.

The teacher may also distribute "Dear Abby" type questions to small groups of students, who must then use the decision-making process to determine a course of action. The group then defends its decision in class. Using sensitive issues commonly faced by teens enlivens the decision-making techniques and shows the relevance they have in their own lives.

Another good discussion topic is considering the alternatives for decisions 2 and 3 on pp. 126-127. Should the woman described in decision 2 go back to the phone company? Try to find a better job? Go on welfare? Cut back her standard of living so she can get by on money from her former husband? Remarry? Use money from the sale of the house to go back to school and train for a higher-paying job?

Should the couple in decision 3 stay where they are? Divorce? Stay married but live in different states, perhaps getting together on weekends? Should the husband move with his wife? Should they apply for other jobs that would be satisfying for both and allow them to live together?

Follow-Up:

The decision-making model should be repeated whenever possible throughout the book.

Resources:

Racosky, Richard. *d+a=R:dreams+action=Reality.* Mount Clemens, Michigan: ActionGraphics Publishing International, 1988.

Gelatt, H. B., Barbara Varenhorst and Richard Carey. *Deciding: A Leader's Guide.* New York: College Entrance Examination Board, 1972.

Future Homemakers of America. *Handbook for Youth-Centered Leadership.* Reston, VA: Future Homemakers of America, 1982.

Its dicussion of the decision-making process includes a "follow-up" section which allows participants to evaluate the effectiveness of their decisions.

Magazine: *Choices, the Magazine for Personal Development and Practical Living Skills*, P.O. Box 640, Lyndhurst, NJ 07071-9985.

Strategies - Decision-Making Patterns

PAGES 134-136 **Workbook 69-71**

Objective:

To help students identify different decision-making patterns and to make them more aware of the ones they use most often.

Presentation Suggestions:

Divide the class into groups of three or four. Ask each group to come up with examples for each pattern. Then bring the class back together and ask each group to share one example for each patten with the others.

Examples:

Wish pattern: You buy a cat hoping it won't affect your allergies.

Escape pattern: You don't try out for chorus because you are afraid someone will laugh at your voice.

Safe pattern: You decide to be a bookkeeper rather than an accountant because you are not sure you will do well in college.

Impulsive pattern: You buy a new outfit with part of your tuition money a week before fees are due.

Fatalistic pattern: You decide to run in a marathon even though your knee hurts when you run.

Compliant pattern: You marry someone because s/he asks you to.

Delaying pattern: You put off reading your history assignments until the night before the final.

Agonizing pattern: You think every item on the menu sounds good and have to keep asking the waiter to give you a few more minutes.

Planning pattern: You decide to marry someone with similar goals and values.

Intuitive pattern: You move to a city you've never visited because you have a feeling you'll like it.

Activities:

Take a poll of how many students currently use each decision-making pattern.

Ask: "After becoming aware of these patterns for making decisions, what are some patterns you would prefer to use now? Are there some not listed here that you could add?"

Follow-Up:

Ask which pattern would be the best to use in most circumstances.

Risk Taking

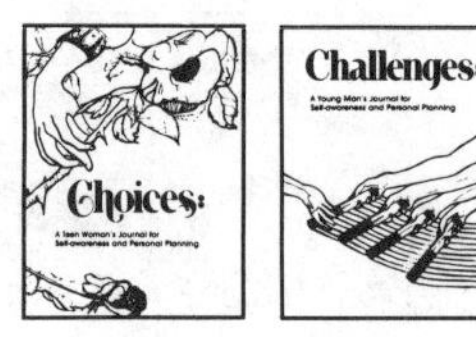

PAGES 137-139 **Workbook 72**

Objective:

To identify the steps of risk taking and the advantages and disadvantages of taking chances.

Presentation Suggestions:

Young women are often unaware of their reluctance to take risks. They may say, "I just don't want to do that," when they actually mean, "I am afraid of failing," or "That's so far away; I can't possibly get there." Young men may the unaware of their reluctance to take certain risks. This model allows students to examine goals and alternatives, break them into components, and evaluate the chance for success.

As a trigger exercise, ask students to complete the sentence, "If I could do anything, I'd . . . ." Students often respond with an action they see as desirable and rewarding, but very risky.

Ask students to think about things they are afraid to do that are not life-threatening. Without necessarily telling what they are afraid of, have them list what could be gained by overcoming the fear and succeeding, and what could happen if they failed. Present a list of common fears among young women, and analyze them in the same way. Some common fears include taking math and science courses, trying out for the school play, newspaper or other activity, competing in an athletic event, talking to unfamiliar people and going to a party alone. For young men, common fears include asking someone for a date, telling a special person how they feel, or defending an unpopular opinion.

Activities:

Ask students to share the entries from their books that concern risks involved in a decision. The class may offer suggestions, encouragement or warnings.

Brainstorm ways in which students feel someone could be encouraged to take a risk: asking, "What's the worst thing that could happen?"; breaking the risk into more manageable parts; approaching the desired action with planned progressive steps; or rewarding yourself for success.

Follow-Up:

When discussing career choice, refer to the section on risk taking. Ask students to rank their three career choices in order of "risk" or "chance for success."

Chapter Six

If yours is a coed class, you've probably noticed a pattern of passivity among the females; a tendency to defer to the males. Assertive behavior among women is still less common than you think, considering the amount of discussion it's received in recent years. This chapter is only an overview, but it should make students aware of their communication patterns. With luck, it will encourage them to become more assertive.

Passivity tends to go along with an inability to make decisions or to take risks. Thus, it can prevent women from going after what they want in life. It is another aspect of the feminine stereotype we are trying to eliminate. The passive woman is "the angel in the house," the person who considers everyone's needs except her own. Some students may think that sounds romantic. We know better.

For young men, passivity can get them in as much trouble as the more common aggressive response. Learning how to stand up to one's own group, gang, or peers, and refusing to join in undesirable behavior or gang like "rites of passage" can keep a young man out of trouble.

You are less likely to find aggressive females in your class. But students should be warned that it is possible to go too far in the opposite direction, and that this behavior can be equally destructive.

This chapter is made to order for a guest speaker. Assertiveness trainers can be found in almost every locality and often do an excellent job of getting their message across to students in an entertaining way.

For the remainder of the course, occasionally point out responses or ask students to identify them as assertive, passive or aggressive.

Aggressive, Assertive or Passive

PAGES 144-145 **Workbook 73**

Objective:

To begin building effective communication skills by learning to identify aggressive, assertive and passive statements and behavior.

Presentation Suggestions:

After explaining the terms (see text), ask students to work through the exercise. Then discuss responses.

Activities:

Invite an outside instructor to present a workshop on assertiveness training. You can probably find a trainer through your local community college or university, a women's center, local women's professional groups, or service organizations.

Divide the class into groups of three. Give each group a different situation, and have each student present to the class an aggressive, assertive or passive response. Have the class identify which response fits which category.

Some possible situations: Someone tries to sell you magazines you don't want over the phone; you would like a salesperson to help you pick out a sweater; a friend makes a remark that hurts your feelings; you'd like your neighbor to keep his dog out of your garden; a friend has not returned the book she borrowed two months ago; the neighbor who agreed to pay you five dollars a week to mow his lawn hasn't paid you for three weeks; the waitress brings you food you didn't order; you don't want the hairdresser to cut more than one inch off your hair; you find someone else sitting in your seat at a concert; a teacher wrongly accuses you of copying someone else's homework.

Resources:

Bloom, Lynn Z., Karen Coburn and Joan Pearlman. *The New Assertive Woman,* New York: Dell Publishing Co., 1975.

Butler, Pamela E. *Self-Assertion For Women..* San Francisco: Canfield Press, a division of Harper and Row, 1981.

Girls Incorporated, *Will Power Won't Power.* New York: Author

Write Your Own Responses

PAGES 146-148 **Workbook 74-76**

Objective:

To practice creating individual assertive, aggressive and passive responses to given situations. Feelings associated with these three methods of communication should also be examined.

Presentation Suggestions:

Precede this exercise with examples and discussion. Role-playing contrived situations works well.

Activities:

Ask students to share their feelings about their own aggressive, assertive or passive responses to situations.

After reading "Truth and Consequences," ask students to share situations in which a conscious decision would be made to be aggressive or assertive.

Examples:

Aggressive:

You come out of a store and find someone trying to steal your bike.
A stranger makes advances to you in a movie theater.

Passive:

A police officer stops you for speeding.
Your mother is waiting up for you when you come home three hours past your curfew.

Ask students what an assertive response might be in the above situations.

Instructor's Notes:

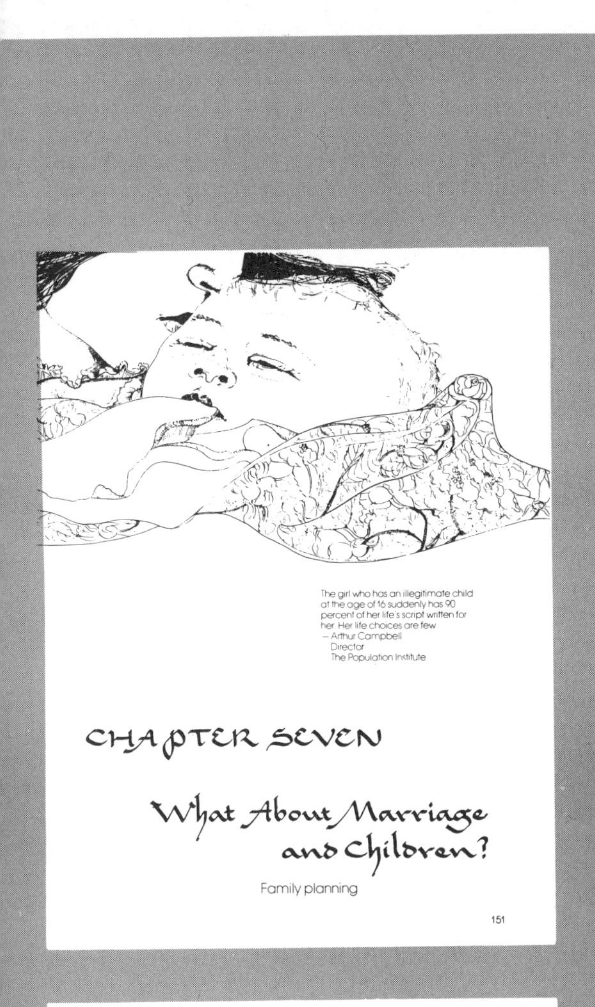
The girl who has an illegitimate child at the age of 16 suddenly has 90 percent of her life's script written for her. Her life choices are few.
— Arthur Campbell
Director
The Population Institute

CHAPTER SEVEN

What About Marriage and Children?

Family planning

151

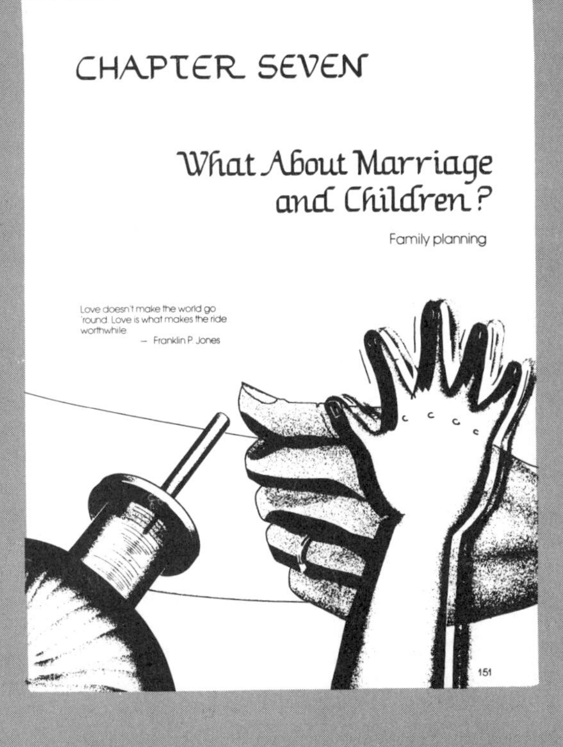
CHAPTER SEVEN

What About Marriage and Children?

Family planning

Love doesn't make the world go 'round. Love is what makes the ride worthwhile.
— Franklin P. Jones

151

Chapter Seven

Teen pregnancy has reached epidemic proportions in many parts of the country. One million teen pregnancies are now reported each year. Forty percent of American women who turned 20 in 1982 had been pregnant at least once.

The reasons for these discouraging statistics are many and varied, but gains can be made simply by talking about the problem. If young people can be made to see the decision to have a child as the tremendous, life-altering one that it is, we will have made some progress.

Little girls have always been intrigued by babies. They tend to develop romantic notions about motherhood. Your job is to help the students develop a more realistic approach to the whole subject. Fortunately, that's not difficult to do.

To show that motherhood is not some ideal state, but a role filled with hardship, disappointment, and limitations as well as fulfillment, you need only make sure that students have some discussions with real-life mothers. There is an exercise that requires them to do this, but you may wish to have some young mothers visit the class as well.

You can also dismantle some myths by presenting the financial implications of parenthood. Stress the cost of pregnancy and childbirth, the cost of supporting a child and the cost of day care, which can effectively obliterate the salary of a woman in a traditional job.

We don't want to appear anti-motherhood, something that might make students disregard anything we have to say. We want to encourage students to think as seriously about this subject as they would about any crucial, life-altering decision; that's exactly what it is.

Young men obviously play an important part in the teen pregnancy picture. They, too, need to understand the results of their actions and the effect on others as well as on themselves.

Another topic that is broached in this chapter is time management and priority setting. It's here because it has so much to do with balancing the roles of spouse, parent and career person. We want to emphasize that, while you may not be able to "have it all," you can certainly have the things that are most important to you, providing you take the time to decide what those things are. To reinforce the principles of time management, you might ask students to list and rank their priorities from time to time for the remainder of the course. Ask students, too, to turn to "Help for the Harried" in Chapter Twelve of the book to see that this is a skill that they will find useful in later years.

The Egg and You

PAGES 153-155 **Workbook 77**

Objective:

To acquaint students with the 24-hour duties and responsibilities a parent has toward a baby.

Presentation Suggestions:

Before handing out the eggs, have students write a description of what they think their first 24 hours at home with a real baby would be like.

When they have completed their papers, be sure to ask if they have included how many times they changed the baby (six to ten times), how they felt physically (soreness, tiredness), how many bottles they sterilized, whether there was soreness due to nursing, and so on. If you haven't had a child, ask a person who has had one to work with the class. Students need a realistic picture of child care, not a glamorous one.

It is a good idea to hard-boil the eggs. If the class is large and mature enough, the teacher can mark one of the eggs with an "A" for an adopted child and one with a "B" for a child with a birth defect. We usually include one set of twins (marked with a "T") in the group.

During the week, students can keep their journals and work through the exercises in this chapter. Often boys will find this exercise is one of the few areas in their lives in which they can demonstrate tenderness.

Most students like doing this exercise and make various beds, cradles or containers for their "babies." They also will decorate their "babies" with faces or distinctive clothing.

Some students do not want to participate at all. Some alternate research projects for these students might be to:

1. Determine the detailed cost of having a child (if not done by the group).
2. Research and prepare a report on child abuse to be presented to the class.
3. Spend one day with a teenage parent and report on the experience.
4. Write a report on teenage pregnancies.

Activities:

During the week, ask students to set their alarm clocks for 1:00 a.m. and 4:00 a.m. one night to get an idea of how it is to get up to feed a baby or tend a sick child.

Ask representatives from local parenting organizations to speak to the class.

Books on parenting such as *The Well Baby Book, Growing Up Free, Baby and Child Care* or others could be shared so the students learn some of the real concerns of parents.

Some classes conduct trials for "child abuse" if something happens to the egg baby. Mike La Manna of Bonita School District, San Dimas, California, allows the class to run the trials and determine the punishment. The punishment consists of a specific number of points taken from the total number possible for the week's assignment.

Some schools use a 10-pound package of flour instead of an egg. While this may be more realistic because of the size and weight, if dropped it is definitely messier than an egg.

Students may interview their own parents and talk about what being a new parent was actually like for them. This can be an eye-opening experience!

Follow-Up:

Ask student to evaluate what they learned during the week by writing a one-page summary of the experience, or have a class discussion.

Ask a Mother
Ask a Father

PAGE 156 **Workbook 78**

Objective:

To personalize communication about child bearing and child rearing, and to provide information students should know before deciding to have children.

Presentation Suggestions:

The exercise should be assigned as homework. You might have a few names handy for students who don't know any new mothers. Is there a teacher or staff person on campus who is a new mother? Any teen parents?

Activities:

Invite a panel of young mothers to come to the class to talk about their experience and answer students' questions.

Having a Child Is Expensive

PAGE 157 Workbook 79

Objective:

To look at the economic realities of child bearing and child rearing.

Presentation Suggestions:

Ask students to research these costs. Suggest they phone obstetricians and hospitals and visit their local department stores to determine the costs of having a child and buying equipment and clothing for a child. As the 1990s begin, the average cost of pregnancy and childbirth is $3,500 and rising.

You might bring copies of Sears', Penny's, or Montgomery Ward's catalogs to class for referral.

What Changes Might Occur if You Were Expecting a Baby?

PAGE 159 Workbook 80

Objective:

To have students consider how their lives would change if they had a child.

Presentation Suggestions:

Ask the students to imagine that they are expecting a baby nine months from now. Ask them to consider how their lives would be different. It often helps to ask them to think of what a day would be like, how a pregnancy would affect their relationships with friends, parents, boyfriend/girlfriend, and the effect it would have on their schooling and career choices.

Activities:

Show the Academy Award-winning film, "Teenage Father," available from Children's Home Society or Planned Parenthood. The film follows a couple involved in a teen pregnancy. Skillfully directed by Taylor Hackford, it is superior to most movies available for school audiences.

Ask a panel of three or four teenage mothers with children between the ages of one and three years to discuss their experiences.

Follow-Up:

Once the students have discussed the problem of having a child in their teen years, ask them to discuss what would be different if they married and financially and emotionally ready to have a child.

This discussion is necessary to emphasize that having a child brings significant changes to a person's life at any age.

Resources:

Foster, Sallie. *One Girl in Ten: Self-Portrait of the Teen-Age Mother*. Claremont, CA: Arbor Press, 1981.

Film:

"Teenage Father," available from the Children's Home Society of California, 1300 West 4th St., Los Angeles, CA 90017. (213) 482-5443.

What Do I Really Want?

PAGE 160 **Workbook 81**

Objective:

To have students consider important issues involving parenthood.

Presentation Suggestions:

Discuss these questions and any others the students might have. Ask them to suggest questions they think should be asked before deciding to be a parent.

Activities:

Invite guest speakers to discuss parenthood.

Possible speakers: member of clergy, marriage and family counselor, panel of single parents, or a recently divorced mother.

What Causes Unplanned Pregnancies?

PAGE 161 **Workbook 82**

Objective:

To encourage students to think about the reasons for unplanned pregnancy so they can consider decisions that might avoid such circumstances. We hope that exposing them to common "lines" they may hear will make them less susceptible to such tactics. The exercise also gives students a chance to think through and practice assertive answers *before* the situation arises.

Presentation Suggestions:

How deeply this issue is discussed depends on the leader, as well as any limitations imposed by other forces.

Activities:

Invite a member of a local community health organization to discuss pregnancy prevention.

List some of the reasons people have children. Discuss which reasons are likely to lead to a happy family situation.

Show "It's Okay to Say 'No Way,'" a music video most appropriate for younger teens. The video encourages "saying no." The presentation is lively, with popular music and dance performed by peers.

Resources:

Dryfoos, Joy G., "Strategies for Prevention of Adolescent Pregnancy: A Personal Quest." *Impact* 83-84. No. 6. Syracuse, New York: Official Publication of the Institution for Family Research and Education, Syracuse University, 1983-84 Edition.

Lindsay, Jeanne. *Teenage Marriage: Coping With Reality*. Buena Park, California: Morning Glory Press, 1988.

Lindsay, Jeanne and Sharon Rodine. *Teen Pregnancy Challenge: Strategies for Change, Book 1*. Buena Park, California: Morning Glory Press, 1989.

Lindsay, Jeanne and Sharon Rodine. *Teen Pregnancy Challenge: Programs for Kids, Book 2*. Buena Park, California: Morning Glory Press, 1989.

Teenage Pregnancy-The Problem That Hasn't Gone Away. The Alan Guttmacher Institute. 360 Park Avenue South, New York, NY 10010, 1981.

Films:

"It's Okay to Say 'No Way!,'" National Board, YWCA of the U.S.A., Program Services Division, 726 Broadway, New York, NY 10003. (212) 614-2700.

"First Things First," 27 minutes. Bill Wadsworth Productions, 1913 W. 37th St., Austin, TX 78731. (512) 478-2971. An award-winning film about teenage relationships that encourages thought and discussion about responsibilities regarding sexual behavior.

Babies Have Fathers Too
Babies Have Mothers Too

PAGE 162 **Workbook 83**

Objective:

To encourage students to begin thinking about characteristics they would like the person they marry to have — characteristics that would most likely lead to a happy relationship.

Presentation Suggestions:

If possible, use the exercise to lead into a discussion of romantic love versus realistic love. How will the student know who the "right" person is for him or her?

Activities:

Ask a group of adults with long-term successful marriages to discuss the traits they have found to be most important in spouses.

The Decision to Have a Child

PAGES 164-165 **Workbook 84**

Objective:

To give students an opportunity to work through the decision-making process when deciding whether or not to have a child.

Presentation Suggestions:

Many young people give more thought to choosing a wardrobe vacation spot than they do to deciding whether to have a child. Urge students to take the matter seriously, to give it a great deal of thought. Emphasize the fact that the decision to have a child soon becomes irrevocable. At what point in their lives will they be willing to live with this decision?

What about Your Goals?

PAGE 166 **Workbook 85**

Objective:

To give students more practice writing goals, especially regarding parenting.

Presentation Suggestions:

Have the class think of possible goals related to parenting and then write action plans (objectives) that could lead to the fulfillment of those goals.

For example, a *goal* might be:

To adopt a child from another culture by the time I'm 30.

Objectives might be:

1. To marry someone who shares my social beliefs.
2. To research adoption agencies and costs before I'm 28.
3. To save $50 a month for adoption and childcare costs, as soon as I get my first job.

Another possible goal:

To concentrate on my career during my twenties, then reevaluate the situation when I'm 30.

Objectives:

1. To learn about and use birth control methods during my twenties.
2. To remain single in my twenties, or marry a man who shares my career goals.
3. To research possible health problems related to late motherhood by my twenty-fifth birthday.

Goal:

To marry and complete my family of two children by age 32. To be a full-time homemaker until the younger child starts school.

Objectives:

1. To marry someone whose career is secure and who can financially support a family of four on one income alone.
2. To work and save every penny possible before the birth of my first child.
3. To research and choose a career that allows me to work part-time with flexible hours.
4. To put off buying a home until after I return to work.

Child Care

PAGE 167 **Workbook 85**

Objective:

To encourage students to think about the relationship between child-care values and career choices.

Presentation Suggestions:

It is important for students to examine their child-rearing values before choosing a career path and becoming a parent.

Discuss possible child-rearing patterns and child-care options in class. Examples include mother staying home with child, father staying home with child, parents working different shifts so that one is always home with child, parents both working part-time and caring for child, using a day-care center, taking the child to a day-care home, having someone come to the home to care for the child, hiring live-in help to care for the child, one or both parents working flexible-hour jobs, one or both parents working in the home.

Ask the class to consider which careers would be most open to flex-time or part-time work. Examples: usually professional or entrepreneurial careers, such as doctors, lawyers, accountants, dietitians, writers, interior designers, craftspeople, consultants, and the like.

Have the class brainstorm in-home opportunities for careers. Examples might be photographers, writers, day-care supervisors, designers, sales representatives, insurance people, hairdressers, caterers, weavers, potters, corporate consultants, typists, tutors and music teachers.

Resources:

Bingham, Mindy and Sandy Stryker. *More Choices: A Strategic Planning Guide for Mixing Career and Family*. Santa Barbara, CA: Advocacy Press, 1987.

Setting Priorities and Making Time

PAGES 169-171 **Workbook 86-87**

Objective:

To teach and illustrate the value of setting priorities and managing time.

Presentation Suggestions:

Review with students the definitions of:

A Priorities = those things that must be done.

B Priorities = those things that *should* be done.

C Priorities = those things that can wait or that don't really have to be done.

Activities:

Ask a person who is married, a parent and career person, to speak on the "superwoman/superman syndrome." What are the speaker's priorities? How are all those roles juggled?

Follow-Up:

A week after students complete their priority chart, discuss the questions at the bottom of the page. Ask if making their task charts and prioritizing helped them complete important tasks. Then ask students to complete the next month's priority chart.

Instructor's Notes:

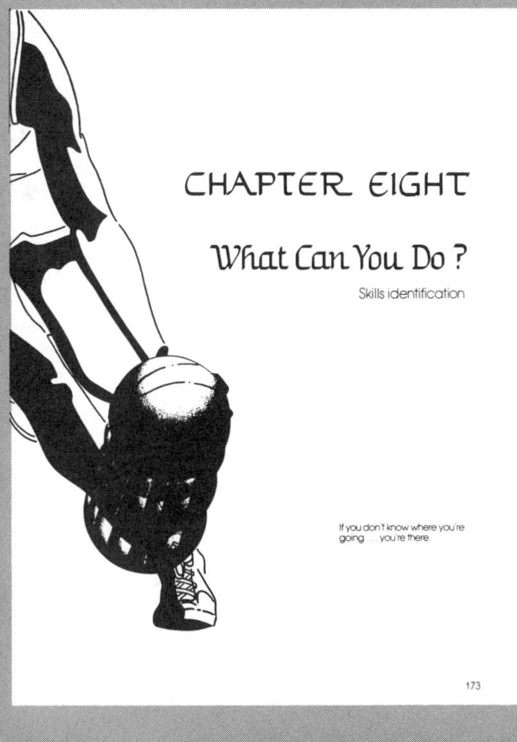

Chapter Eight

Identifying their own skills can be difficult for young people. They may also tend to be modest about admitting to special talents or skills.

To counter ill-conceived modesty and practice assertiveness, you might ask each student to announce to the class what skill or talent each has. ("I make terrific chocolate chip cookies," or "I'm a whiz at math.")

You will also want to discuss "interest" or aptitude tests with your students during the course of this chapter. If your school does not normally give these tests, you may be able to arrange for students to take them. The tests may be particularly valuable because they may be able to detect skills or interests that students themselves are too young or inexperienced to know about. They may encourage students to explore fields they haven't thought about before.

Be sure to explain the difference between an aptitude and an interest. An aptitude is a natural talent or ability. It is something one is good at or has the potential to be good at. Interests are simply what one enjoys. It is possible to be interested in something for which one has no aptitude or to have an aptitude for something in which one has no interest. However, more often than not, we all tend to enjoy what we do well.

Aptitude tests may measure mental or physical abilities. Generally, mental aptitude tests measure verbal ability, math ability and reasoning. Physical aptitude tests, such as the General Aptitude Test Battery, measure twelve kinds of physical aptitude, including finger dexterity and manual dexterity.

Two interest inventories that we have used are the Kuder and the COPs (addresses are on "Job Skills" page). The Kuder asks students to choose which of three activities they like most and which they like least. These answers determine basic career categories that might be suitable (outdoors, mechanical, etc.). The COPs test asks students to rate their feelings about each given statement ("like a lot" to "don't like at all"). It also determines job categories, then goes on to list specific jobs that fit the student's profile.

Remind students that their lists of skills will continue to grow throughout their lives. Ask them to look at the "Filling the Gaps" and "My Retirement" exercises in Chapter Twelve to see how their skills will be a continued source of enjoyment.

This chapter encourages students to "Experience What You Can." We hope that you will encourage them, too. Perhaps you could have a class discussion of activities in the school, or in the area, which could provide new experiences to students and which are neither too expensive nor too dangerous. Or students could think of three things they have wanted to do, but have been afraid to try. Is there a real reason why they should not, or could not, do them? If not, they might practice goal setting by writing the objectives which could lead to the desired experience.

What Are Your Skills?

PAGES 175-176 **Workbook 88**

Objective:

To make students aware of the skills they already possess.

Presentation Suggestions:

Identifying skills is very difficult for students. We attempt to make it easier by focusing on activities they already do in school and at home.

"What Are Your Skills?" Activity Chart

To introduce the exercise, write some sample activities on the blackboard. For example:

Activity
cooking

Skills
measuring
working with hands
organizing
attending to detail

Likes
creating
making something good to eat
pleasing others
working with hands

Environment
indoors

Talk with students as they complete this section to help them determine what it is about each activity that they really like and what skills may be involved. Students need to realize they are already capable of doing many things.

Activities:

Ask students to list their skills.

Choose jobs/careers and, as a group, discuss the skills that would be needed for each.

Examples:

Secretary: Typing, word processing, organizing, listening

Surgeon: Finger dexterity, science aptitude, learning ability, study skills

Lawyer: Verbal aptitude, reasoning ability, researching ability, writing

Best Subjects

PAGE 177 **Workbook 89**

Objective:

To have students focus on school subject matter and decide why they like or dislike a class. This could help them become aware of abilities they may have.

Presentation Suggestions:

Stress that the student is evaluating subject content and not the teacher.

Job Skills

PAGE 178 **Workbook 89**

Objective:

To enable the students to begin a job skills inventory.

Presentation Suggestions.

Using the chalkboard, list one or two students' skills and ask for ideas on how the skills might translate into job or career training.

Speaking, writing — lawyer, politician, journalist, teacher

Selling, math, talking to people — real estate salesperson, marketing specialist, industrial salesperson, financial planner

Puzzle solving, organizing — computer programmer, engineer, scientist

You might ask what skills are desirable in any job.

Activities:

If one of the students knows someone who wants to re-enter the workforce, list that person's skills and have the class brainstorm possible jobs.

This is a good time to give an interest inventory. We use either Kuder or the COPS (see chapter introduction).

Resources:

Kudor: Science Research Associates, 1540 Page Mill Road, Palo Alto, CA 94304.

COPs: California Occupational Preference System, Edits, P.O. Box 7234,
San Diego, CA 92107.

Chapter Nine

Here *Choices* and *Challenges* take slightly different directions, and some of the exercises and stories are different. Young women are asked to examine the possibilities and the benefits of nontraditional careers. Young men are asked to examine the benefits to themselves and their future families of encouraging the women in their lives to pursue a career that can support a family or add to the financial security of the family in a meaningful way.

The entire book has been building to the next two chapters. We hope that by this time, students have learned that they will need to support themselves and that they *can* do just that, but that living is expensive. We hope they realize that the way in which they develop the blueprint for the next forty-five years, namely, through their education, will pay dividends for the rest of their lives.

Ask a Career Woman
Ask the Man Who Knows

PAGES 183-184

PAGE 183

Workbook 90-91

Objective:

To give students an opportunity to meet and talk with career people who might become role models. Students will also practice using interview techniques and gain more realistic views of working life.

Presentation Suggestions:

You might need to have a few names on hand for students who don't know career people, particularly career women. Perhaps your friends and co-workers will help. Or obtain names from a local professional organization, Chamber of Commerce, or the United Way.

Activities:

It is vitally important to invite guest speakers who are role models and can share their experiences with the class. The young women in particular need to meet people they can relate to in jobs that are not traditionally female. Young men need to meet men with nontraditional careers and lifestyles.

If a female student has never seen a woman engineer, plumber, legislator or physicist, she is not as likely to realize that these are all possibilities for her. The same is true for the young men in your class. Be sure to invite male role models who have chosen careers traditionally held by women. It is important for you to find some of these people and bring them into your classroom. The more, the better. The wider variety of occupations represented, the more options your students will see for themselves. You can also invite college-age students, who are currently preparing for nontraditional careers, to come and speak to the group. Being closer in age to the student, they are received well.

Resources:

Michelson, Maureen R., ed. *Women & Work: Photographs and Personal Writings.* Pasadena, California: NewSage Press, 1986. (P.O. Box 41029, Pasadena, CA 91114.)

Film:

"Sandra, Zella, Dee and Claire: Four Women in Science," 19 minutes. EDC/WEEA Publishing Center, 55 Chapel Street, Suite 200, Newton, MA 02160. (800) 225-3088.

Note to Instructor

At this point in class, assign pp. 184-189 to be read independently. You may need to help the young men work through the "A Place of Your Own" exercise (instructions follow). Then, break the class into groups of three (boys together, girls together) to discuss what they read and list comments, to be voiced by a spokesperson for each group. You can begin the discussion by explaining the general content of the chapter in each book to the whole class. Then the boys will know that the girls are reading about nontraditional careers; the girls will know the boys' material covered new partnerships. Begin with the small group comments and reports and lead into a general discussion.

Questions for discussion might include:

1. What are the advantages of a non-traditional career for girls?
2. What are the advantages to young men if their spouses pursue non-traditional careers?
3. How do students feel about the salary difference between traditionally male and female jobs?
4. Do they think women face discrimination in the job market and in schools? If so, what should be done about it?
5. What problems might be expected to occur when both the husband and wife work outside the home?
6. What qualities might be helpful in dealing with changing roles in a marriage?

More Activities:

Form a debate team (at least one male and one female on each side) to debate the Equal Rights Amendment.

Ask students to form a panel to debate the question, "Should traditionally male jobs pay more money than traditionally female jobs?"

With the class brainstorm reasons why salaries for women's jobs historically have been less than those for men's jobs.

Ask the students to multiply the salaries at the bottom of p. 189 by 30 years to demonstrate what this difference is over a 30-year working life.

A Place of Your Own

PAGE 187 **Workbook 92**

Objective:

To demonstrate the total family income required to purchase a home in most areas of the United States today. Also to point out the probable necessity for two incomes of substantial size to purchase a home. (As noted previously, the majority of high-paying jobs are traditionally male jobs.)

Presentation Suggestions:

Ask the young men in your class probably the young women in your class, too, even though they don't have this exercise in their book to complete this exercise. It might be best to complete it together as a class. Then ask the students to turn back to p. 63 and review their desired housing and its cost. Where does this fit on the scale of required income? Can they purchase this home on one income? Do the young women need to consider a traditionally male job to make the purchase of a home possible?

The Importance of Math

PAGES 190-192 **No Workbook Page**

Objective:

To impress upon the students the fact that math is *mandatory* for most high-paying professions.

Presentation Suggestions:

Discuss the math history of your class. How many students did well in math in grade school? How many do well in it now? How many are interested in it? How many are not? Why do they think changes have occurred?

If your class is typical, the young women in your class are probably planning to take as little math as possible. You need to change their minds. Discuss "Math Anxiety" in young women and what that usually unfounded anxiety costs in future earning power. What are ways of overcoming the "fear"? How has society given young women the feeling that they do not need math?

Activities:

Have students look at college catalogues to determine the math requirements for different majors.

Compare the list of job salaries on p. 85 with the college major chart on p. 191. Identify which majors lead to which careers. Then compare the salary levels of the careers requiring math with the salary levels of those not requiring math.

Identify the math tutoring resources at your high school.

See pp. 140-147 in *More Choices* for more exercises.

Form a "Math Mentor" club where students who are good at math make a commitment to help other students who need guidance.

Resources:

Bingham, Mindy and Sandy Stryker. *More Choices: A Strategic Planning Guide for Mixing Career and Family.* Santa Barbara, CA: Advocacy Press, 1987.

Skolnick, Joan, Carol Langbort and Lucille Day. *How To Encourage Girls in Math and Science: Strategies for Parents and Educators.* Palo Alto, CA: Dale Seymour Publications, 1982.

Kaseberg, Alice, Nancy Kreinberg and Diane Downie. *Equals.* Berkeley, CA: Lawrence Hall of Science, 1980.

"Mathematical Sex Differences—It's in the Numbers." *Science News,* 118, December 13, 1980, p. 372.

Lockheed, M., Thorpe, M., Brooks-Gunn, J. and McAloon, A. *Sex and Ethnic Differences in Middle School Mathematics Science and Computer Science: What Do We Know?* Princeton, New Jersey: Educational Testing Service, 1985.

Are You Giving up a High-Paid Future for a Part-Time Job?

PAGE 193 **Workbook 92**

Objective:

To help students realize that future considerations must be a factor in decisions they are making now. Does a short-term advantage take precedence over a long-term disadvantage?

Presentation Suggestions:

How much emphasis you place on the topic of part-time jobs will depend on your class. If the majority of your students either do not work or *must* work, there is no need to go into the subject deeply. But, if you sense that some of your students are not paying enough attention to their school work because they are working to acquire spending money with which they might be frivolous, then bring up the topic for an interesting discussion.

Be sensitive to the feelings of students who may need to work. If there are some in your class, discuss how high school math and science courses may be taken in a community college before starting more demanding math/science majors. It may take longer to complete their education, but it will be worth it in the long run.

Activities:

Review hourly job rates on p. 81 and discuss conversion to annual salaries so students can easily determine annual salaries themselves!

Brainstorm entry level or part-time jobs a student might find that would be beneficial to a professional career.

You must do the thing you think you cannot do.
— Eleanor Roosevelt

If you can do it then why do it?
— Gertrude Stein

CHAPTER TEN

Putting It All Together

Career planning

195

CHAPTER TEN

Putting It All Together

Career planning

If a man loves the labor of his trade, apart from any question of success or fame, the gods have called him.
— Robert Louis Stevenson

Happiness is liking what you do as well as doing what you like.

195

Chapter Ten

At last students are ready to research specific careers that they think right be suitable for them. Remind them to consider their values, goals, interests and skills before choosing the jobs. You can get an idea of how much students have teamed about themselves and the real world by which choices they make. If young women still want to be like Cinderella, you may have to quickly review the purpose of the class.

We ask that the girls choose one job from a list of nontraditional careers on p. 200 or any other list of nontraditional jobs. We hope that even if choices one and two are "nurse" and "secretary," looking closely at alternate careers will pique their curiosity. Remind students too that there are *thousands* of different jobs. Most of us are aware of only a few of them. You might bring an *Occupational Outlook Handbook* to class (borrow it from the school library), or a book like *The American Almanac of Jobs and Salaries* by John W. Wright, available at bookstores. Pass the books around, or read from them at random. This should raise consciousness and help students think beyond the obvious.

Students are also asked to hold informational interviews with people currently working in the fields they have decided to research. You may need to help students locate people to interview. Names are available from phone books, labor unions, librarians, the Chamber of Commerce, employment agencies, professional organizations, and so on. Particularly for young women students, if there is a professional women's network in the area, ask for its directory. Often women are listed by career as well as by name. These women should be particularly willing to help your students. Passing the directory around the class may be another way of demonstrating the wide variety of jobs available for both men and women.

Emphasize that, along with choosing a marriage partner and deciding to have children, choosing a career is a decision that will determine much of their future lives. Career research is also a skill that can be used later in life. Ask students to look at the "I've Decided to Change Careers" exercise in Chapter Twelve.

Who Are You Anyway?

PAGE 196 **Workbook 93**

Objective:

To summarize what students have learned about themselves while working through the book.

Presentation Suggestions:

Assist the students by listing the page number in the book where they can find their previous responses in the various categories:

Skills — 176-178

Family Goals — 166

Values — 103-105

Goals — 112-113, 139

Interest Inventories or Aptitude Tests

Discuss the importance of creating a "picture" of themselves and stress the need to consider all the categories whenever career choices are made.

Activities:

An art project works well as a supplement to this exercise. Some possibilities are drawing trees or flowers, with the categories making up branches and petals. A collage with a recent photograph of the student personalizes the experience and helps an individual consider the exercise seriously.

Follow-Up:

Suggest that students repeat this "picture" at different points in their lives, such as when they graduate from high school, start college, change a career, and so forth.

Job Characteristics

PAGE 197 **Workbook 93**

Objective:

To ask students to evaluate choices in job characteristics that should be made before beginning career research.

Presentation Suggestions:

Ask students to list what they *value* in each of the four job characteristics areas listed.

Activities:

Form small groups to brainstorm job titles that match those four choices. Someone who circled "Outdoors," "Own Boss," "High Pay," "Machines," might consider being:

A contractor

A free-lance photographer

An architect

A veterinarian

A construction equipment sales representative

A manager of a large mechanized farm

Everyone Can't Be a Superstar

PAGES 198-199 **Workbook 94**

Objective:

To make students aware of the vast array of exciting career opportunities available beyond the "obvious" jobs.

Presentation Suggestions:

This is a good brainstorming exercise for the class. Ask them to add to each superstar's list. Then go over each job with a brief description of what the job entails. Emphasize the thousands of jobs people don't normally think about. (see chapter introduction). Talk about such jobs as store owner, veterinarian, YWCA director, and the like. What kinds of people might be happy in these careers?

Activities:

The Corporate Game. This activity is a one-day class and could be facilitated by a guest speaker from the corporate world.

At this point in the course, students have some indication of the areas that they wish to pursue for a career/vocation. The teacher asks students to state what career/vocation they hope to follow. As students respond, the teacher must remember or make a note of each. The teacher then tells the students that they, collectively, have money to start a business. It can be a service industry or a manufacturing business. The students decide what it is that they want to provide or manufacture. Students choose a name for their company. The teacher then explains how companies are structured. As each position is identified, a student from the class fits into the role. This exercise helps them visualize the structure and responsibilities in a company, and it stresses the need for flexibility. Many will have to adapt their skills in the workplace. For example, the auto-machine worker will be building shoe manufacturing machinery, the restaurant owner will be operating the staff dining room and working in public relations with clients and buyers, the chiropractor will be designing car seats and doors, the computer programmer will be managing the accounting department, the realtor will be needed to help relocate and expand the business, and the pilot will operate the company's private planes. As company shareholders, they will all benefit from their hard work and creativity.

Gathering Job Information

PAGES 200-205 **Workbook 95-100**

Objective:

To help students find pertinent information about careers and to have them learn how to begin a career research process.

Presentation Suggestions:

Before beginning the research, read each of the twelve questions aloud and explain each item with examples.

If a career center is nearby, arrange for a tour or a presentation to acquaint students with available resources. Libraries have some career information, such as the *Occupational Outlook Handbook* and *Dictionary of Occupational Titles*. There are also books about individual careers or career clusters, such as careers in the arts, business and so forth.

Depending on the abilities of the students, the research can be done as homework or by taking the entire class to the career center or library. When taking the class, the teacher is available to assist students with their research.

It may take three days to complete the research. Those who finish early can examine college catalogues or look for information about specific training programs or vocational schools.

Activities:

When research is finished, ask the school's career guidance counselor to speak to the class about opportunities within the school for internships and further training.

Guest speakers are vital to this section of the course. If possible, ask students for a list of careers that interest them. Be sure to include representatives from nontraditional careers.

Some speakers will have very definite ideas about what they wish to communicate to students. Most will ask you for some guidance. We stress their impact as role models and give only a few suggestions to help speakers personalize their remarks and keep student interest. We ask guests to think about themselves at age 14, 15, or 16 and tell what they thought they wanted out of life then, and what actually happened. Students need to hear about people adjusting and making changes. This beginning really seems to help the students and speakers relate to one another. We also ask the speaker to describe his/her training for the job. What does he/she enjoy and dislike about it? An example of a typical day is also useful.

Speakers should also be aware that students are often interested in the balance between career life and family life. Most students are eager to ask questions of the speaker, but, if the group is particularly passive or reticent, written questions can be used.

Major corporations, vocational schools, and the military all have speakers who will come to classrooms and give presentations about a variety of career opportunities. Although they will all speak about their particular school, business, or branch of service, they often give a great deal of general information. A representative from a school of fashion design, for instance, will often describe the entire fashion industry, explaining types of jobs involved. Career magazines, such as "Real World" provide up-to-date information about the world of work.

Field trips to workplaces and universities or colleges are enjoyable, motivational experiences. They can provide the spark that encourages a young person to make the decision to really "go for" a new goal.

Boy Scouts:

The Explorer Career Awareness Program offers seminars in high schools, and coordinate speakers in areas identified by the students. This program could be utilized to complement the *Choices/Challenges* course.

In addition, the Explorer program offers Explorer Posts in some communities in specific career areas, e.g., fire fighting, computer programming, law enforcement, retail trade, and so forth. Male and female students can join these posts for a year-long, in-depth study of a particular career. Contact your local Boy Scout Council for more information.

Resources:

Ricci, Larry J. *High Paying Blue-Collar Jobs for Women.* New York: Ballantine Books, 1981.

Wright, John W. *The American Almanac of Jobs and Salaries*, revised ed. New York: Avon Books, 1987.

Magazine: "Real World." King Features Syndicate, Inc., 235 East 45th Street, New York, NY 10017. (212) 455-4000.

Occupational Outlook Handbook, U.S. Department of Labor, Bureau of Labor Statistics.*

Occupational Outlook Quarterly, U.S. Department of Labor, Bureau of Labor Statistics.*

Monthly Labor Review, U.S. Department of Labor, Bureau of Labor Statistics.*

* Available in libraries.

Ask An Expert

PAGES 206-207 **Workbook 101**

Objective:

To give students an opportunity to practice interview techniques and have them learn the value of obtaining firsthand information about a career.

Presentation Suggestions:

The instructor may need to assist the student in locating a person in the chosen field (see introduction to chapter).

Review the proper interviewing etiquette with students. Advise them to come to the point of the interview quickly and not to take up much time.

Activities:

One of the best ways to acquaint a student with a particular career is to have the student visit someone at a job site. This process is often called "shadowing." Many people are willing to take a half hour of their time to meet with interested students and conduct a tour of their workplace. See *Career Choices: A Guide for Teens and Young Adults: Who Am I? What Do I Want? How Do I Get It?* by Mindy Bingham and Sandy Stryker for details on arranging for a shadowing experience.

Your Goals

PAGE 209 **Workbook 102**

Objective:

To have students write specific goals.

Presentation Suggestions:

This exercise may be expanded into a two-year plan.

Activities:

Students should include at some point, in either their two-year plan or as a separate exercise in the class, a schedule of classes they intend to take for their high school years. If they are seniors, they should include a timetable of things to be done for post-secondary training, like determining when they need to apply for college, submit financial aid forms, and so on. The teacher should provide a list of classes required for high school graduation and admission requirements for state colleges and universities.

Note: This is a good point to have students complete another "Envision Your Life" exercise from Chapter One. You will be able to determine what impact the class has had by comparing the "before" and "after" charts.

Instructor's Notes:

Chapter Eleven

We all know that the cost of higher education is skyrocketing, that jobs are hard to get, especially for teens, and that funds for financial assistance have been cut in many areas. Yet, aid is available, although much of it is based primarily on need. Scholarships and grants can be found for students with outstanding academic achievement or for those possessing particular skills or interests. Many fraternal or professional organizations offer financial aid to the children of their members. Some businesses are prepared to help the children of their employees. Encourage students to explore every avenue.

Also, more colleges are offering degrees that can be earned entirely at night, allowing students to hold down full-time jobs as well as attend classes. Many businesses pay a portion or all of the tuition for classes taken by their employees. On-campus jobs are available to students in need of financial assistance. Low-interest loans are still available.

This is one chapter that lends itself to the lecture format. Provide students with as much information as you can about the various kinds of schools, their advantages and disadvantages. Talk about relative costs and sources for financial aid. Be certain to stress that post-high school education is extremely flexible. Students don't have to go to college full-time for four years immediately after high school. There are older students, part-time students, special students, night school students, independent study students, and so on. You might consider quizzing students on these answers. You need to be sure students understand it.

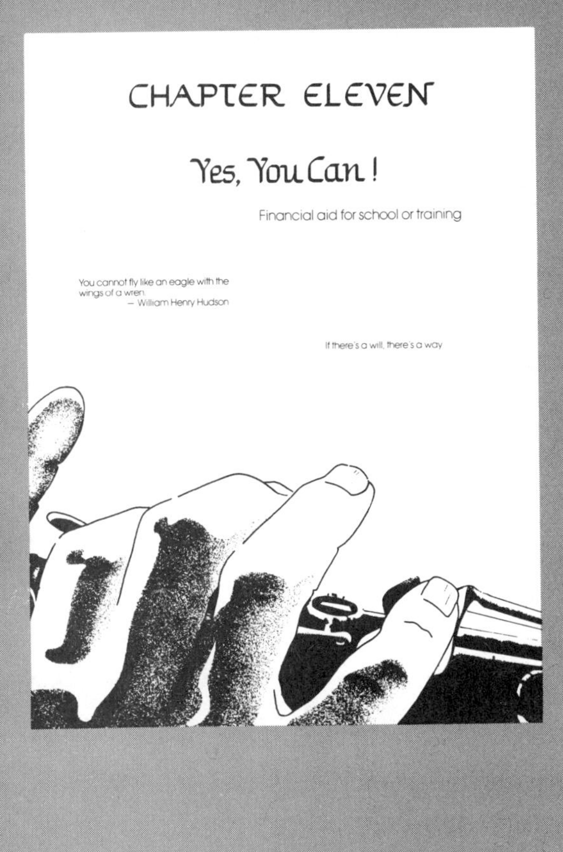

Estimated Expenses and Resources

PAGE 213 **Workbook 103**

Objective:

To help students prepare a budget to determine the cost of attending college or a training school of their choice.

Presentation Suggestions:

Most students do not know the differences between a two-year school, state college, university, private school, vocational school or apprenticeship program. These differences need to be explained either by the teacher with the use of catalogs or by a panel of representatives from different institutions.

Activities:

Ask a school counselor or local college counselor to give a presentation on financial aid.

Invite a junior or senior from a college or university to speak on her/his experiences.

Visit a college campus for a tour.

Resources:

Hagener, Karen C., ed. *Peterson's: The College Money Handbook.* Princeton, NJ: Peterson's Guides, 1983.

Keeslar, Oreon. *Financial Aids for Higher Education: A Catalogue for Undergraduates*. Dubuque, IA: Wm. C. Brown Publishers, 1984.

Lever, William Edward. *How to Obtain Money for College.* New York: Arco Publishing Company, Inc., 1978.

Peterson's Four Year Colleges. Princeton, NJ: Peterson's Guides, 1984.

Straughn, Charles and Barbarasue Lovejoy Straughn. *Lovejoy's College Guide*. New York: Monarch Press, 1983.

Chapter Twelve

We hope that, as you've gone through the book, you've directed students to exercises in this chapter in which the skills they've been using will be used in later life. We want to emphasize that the skills they've developed are not to be forgotten. People who have know their values and goals, who are assertive, independent, skilled, are people whose lives will be filled with myriad choices and challenges.

What Are You Doing for the Rest of Your Life?

PAGES 217-238 **Workbook 103**

Exercises for the Future:

The skills learned in values clarification goal and objective setting, decision making, assertiveness, priority setting and skills identification will empower the individual to make wise choices.

Presentation Suggestions:

Although students will not complete this section until later stages in life, review each exercise to acquaint them with the skills they will need to recall in each situation.

> If you have chosen to complete the *Choices* and *Challenges* curriculum in a nine week or quarter time frame, why not use the *More Choices* curriculum for your second nine weeks of the semester?

Using Choices and Challenges in Various Settings

Choices and *Challenges* are used in a variety of settings and as part of widely different programs. Some of these include:

Career Education Classes

Guidance and Planning Programs

Family Life/On Your Own/Home Economics Classes

Decision-Making Classes

Independent Study Classes

Orientation Classes

English Classes

Pregnant Teens/Parenting Programs

Vocational Readiness Programs

Home Room Programs

Individual Counseling Programs

Group Counseling Programs

Girls Clubs /Boys Clubs Programs

Y.W.C.A./Y.M.C.A. Programs

Girls Scouts/Boy Scouts Programs

Big Sister /Big Brother Programs

4-H/Future Farmers of America

National Charity League Programs

Juvenile Justice Programs

Many professional organizations work together with schools or community groups to organizes special programs. The Business and Professional Women and the American Association of University Women are two that have taken active roles in helping to implement the programs. Organizations that may be able to help in your community are discussed under ***Resources***.

Some Sample Curricula

CAREER EDUCATION

In Santa Barbara, we teach the curriculum in a nine-week quarter class called Career Planning. The quarter class paired with Career Planning in our school is Driver Education. Since these are the only two quarter classes offered, and Driver Education is a very popular class, most students take Career Planning. The majority of students in these classes are sophomores and their abilities range from low to very high.

Each class situation is different and demands flexibility on the part of the teacher. But we feel the following exercises are essential in any program:

Working World

Women in the Workforce Quiz

Budget

Values Survey

Goal Setting

Family Planning

Career Research

The Budget Exercise is the key element in the curriculum. It answers the question, "Why should I be concerned about any of these issues?" In our nine-week format, the budget usually takes one week (five class periods) and follows the introductory materials about attitudes and sex-role stereotyping. Once we have students' interest through completion of the budget, the curriculum follows naturally. Or, put another way, once students realize they need to start preparing for their future, the rest of the curriculum shows them how.

Other key elements in a career education curriculum include exposure to as many role models as possible. While many young women believed that a woman can be an engineer, they are less likely to see that "I" can be an engineer. Role models who obviously enjoy their careers become invaluable in assisting students to make that personal connection.

In reaching their goals, teens are often unaware of ways to pursue post-secondary training or education. Many know little of what is available to them. A lecture on such opportunities-vocational schools, two-year colleges, state and private universities, apprenticeship programs, and so forth should be incorporated into the curriculum. Guest speakers can provide much information in these areas.

In many schools, as in ours, The Egg and You exercise from the chapter on marriage and children is part of a home economics class. We still feel the chapter is essential, but we do not do the egg baby exercise. Instead we show the film "Teenage Father" on one day and discuss the topic on another. Basically we talk about the *realistic* ways in which having a child affects a person's life, and ask each student to consider the consequences.

Other optional topics include those relating to job-seeking skills such as resume writing and teaming effective interview techniques.

As a general guideline, we spend approximately the following number of days on each topic.

Chapter 1-2	1 1/2 weeks
Chapter 3	1 week
Chapter 4	1 week
Chapter 5	3 days
Chapter 6	1 day
Chapter 7	2 days
Chapter 8	1 day
Chapter 9	1 day
Chapter 10	3 days
Chapter 11	1 day
Chapter 12	2 days
Interest surveys and job selection	3 days
College and post-secondary training	1 day
Resumes and interviews	3 days
Guest speakers	4-5 days

The *Choices/Challenges* curriculum can be a lot of fun to teach. It is one of the few times individualized teaching is not only possible, but encouraged.

ENGLISH

At Laguna Beach High School, Jan Fritzen, counselor, and Charles Schiller, English teacher, team teach a tremendously popular trimester English class, taken mostly by seniors. The following description of the program is provided by the two instructors.

"THE WRITING STRAND"

Both the process of writing and the final written work help to drive home the concepts of the *Choices and Challenges* curriculum. The sense of community fostered by considering these basic questions together is also encouraged by the group's involvement in each person's work.

The writing process begins with pre-writing activities — discussion, brainstorming, fluency writing-which are suited to help students react to, clarify, and expand the ideas generated by the text. Sharing in pairs or small groups also helps to build ideas.

Every chapter in the text profits from discussion; some lead more naturally than others to writing. The transition from discussion to writing is made easy with a technique called "clustering," recording the ideas of a brainstorming discussion in clusters on the board. Looking at this visual record of the discussion makes it easy to write about.

(Similarly, a good way to help students focus on guest speakers or lyrics of popular music or a film is to use a "Reaction Brief" form that asks for a one-page essay based on the ideas just encountered. See the example that follows.)

If a more developed assignment is being worked on, strategies designed to focus and order the writing come next. The technique of the "Set-Up" asks students to write a thesis statement, briefly list supporting ideas, and then prepare a sentence concluding for the eventual paper. A rubric or set of criteria for evaluating the final paper is useful at this point to guide the preparation of the paper and later to take the mystery out of teacher evaluation. The rough draft is based on the set-up and it too benefits from sharing with other students to get their reactions and suggestions for possible revision.

Editing, which can also be done in pairs or small groups, is followed by preparation of the final copy and teacher evaluation.

Some sample assignments for such a writing strand include major papers (approximately 500 words) on the students' personal philosophies of finance (Chapter Three), the autobiographical essay required for many scholarship applications (Chapter Eleven), and the analysis of the problems and solutions suggested by relevant literature (such as the novel *Ordinary People*).

If the students are planning to attend college, another source of relevant topics is the essay required by many private colleges in their application packets. This assignment can be profitably expanded by asking a local college to supply a set of application forms, having the students complete the writing, and then inviting the admissions officer to speak to the class about how these essays are evaluated when they reach the college.

The admissions officer could also bring samples of real application essays and then guide the students in evaluating them as an admissions committee would.

For an English class, supplemental reading should be assigned from a reading list related to the course content. The following represents the beginning of the list that is in the process of being developed.

A Doll's House by Henrik lbsen

Death of a Salesman by Arthur Miller

Ordinary People by Judith Guest

Outrageous Acts and Everyday Rebellions by Gloria Steinem

Biographies

PLANNING AND GUIDANCE

The Bonita Unified School District uses *Choices and Challenges* as the basis of an eighteen-week semester course called Planning and Guidance. The class is required for all tenth grade students, and the teachers work closely with the counselors in helping students plan their high school programs, as well as work through the curriculum

Mike La Manna, a teacher at Bonita High School, shares a sample syllabus below.

Grading: Accumulation of Points

Class participation (individual and group)	5 points/day
Daily class assignments	5 points/day
Journal	20 points/week
Paper on "You"	100 points

Extra credit — (only for a student who is earning an A, B, or C)

Materials needed daily-three-ring notebook, pen or pencil, your brain and an open, thinking mind!

Suggestions for Extra Credit: (If you have other suggestions, see teacher.)

a. Five magazine or newspaper articles, cartoons, current events, etc. (5 points)

b. Book report on related topic (1 points)

c. Synopsis and critique of related TV program (5 points)

d. Music analysis (with written lyrics) (5 points)

Tentative Topics to Be Explored:

The total you	COPs test
Decision making	Assertiveness
Careers	Sexuality
Family	Sex roles and identity
Your future	Goal setting
Communication	Two-year high school plan
Values	Dating
Budget	Parenting

While each teacher teaches the class differently, some general goals, objectives and evaluative criteria are included here for your reference.

Goal Statements for Planning and Guidance:

1. To stimulate students to begin thinking about their futures and practice stretching their imaginations.
2. To encourage students to examine their attitudes about sex roles and to make students aware of the unconscious associations of sex with jobs and sex-role stereotyping.
3. To encourage students to communicate with people close to them who influence their attitudes.
4. To make student aware of women's contributions to society and to point out that in our society masculine characteristics may be valued more highly than feminine characteristics.
5. To have the students internalize the need for careful planning for their futures.
6. To make students aware of unexpected events that actually do happen in life.
7. To help students realize what income they will need to live as they would like at age 28, and to awaken them to the fact that to achieve that income, career preparedness should begin in their teens.
8. To have students discern some of the values most important to them.
9. To have students learn to write specific objectives that, when put together, make a step-by-step action plan toward completing a goal.
10. To help students identify different decision-making patterns.
11. To practice creating individual assertive, aggressive and passive responses to given situations.
12. To personalize communication about child bearing and child rearing and to provide information students should consider when deciding to have children.
13. To give students practice in writing goals and coming up with action plans to meet them.
14. To have students look at the issue of setting priorities and managing time to achieve those priorities.
15. To help students find pertinent information about careers and to have them learn how to begin career research process.

Objectives and Evaluative Criteria:

1. By the end of the semester, all students will have had the opportunity to establish specific objectives which create an action plan toward completing a goal.
2. Students will have knowledge and will be able to proceed properly toward applying and securing career goal.
3. Students will have the ability to identify different decision-making patterns and to practice creating individual assertive, aggressive and passive responses with 90 percent accuracy.
4. By the end of the semester, 90 percent of the students will be capable of setting individual priorities and managing their time to achieve those priorities.
5. By the end of the semester, at least 85 percent of the students will be able to demonstrate effective communication skills with their peers, their parents and their prospective employers.
6. Students will have knowledge of and will be able to discern the responsibilities of parenting and the rearing of children.

Areas Most Commonly Adapted to the Curriculum:

HOME ECONOMICS

The life and family planning aspects of the *Choices/Challenges* curriculum make these books naturals for use in home economics classes. The budget is of value to those who will soon be living on their own, as well as to those who will be caring for a family. This section also helps students clarify their educational and career goals.

The plans completed by each student serve as an individual guide and also help parents, teachers and counselors do what they can to see that students achieve their goals. Students also learn to assess physical and emotional risks that may be involved in their present or future activities and clearly see the possible consequences, both positive and negative. The curriculum has proved itself valuable in both pregnancy prevention and drop-out prevention.

VOCATIONAL EDUCATION

Choices and *Challenges* make an important contribution to vocational education by helping students discover the relationship between lifestyle and career selection. Students first gain better understanding of "the high cost of living" and analyze the average annual salaries of different careers. As a result, they become more determined to complete their high school education and go on to train in the field of their choice. The books encourage students to take advanced math classes and to consider "nontraditional" careers. They also offer information on various kinds of post-high school education, and how to go about financing it.

Each state has a GENDER EQUITY COORDINATOR funded by the Carl Perkins Vocational Education Act. The coordinators have federal monies to fund programs throughout their states. If you are looking for funding to start a *Choices/Challenges, Changes* or *More Choices* program in your school, they are a good resource to contact. Their offices are in your state Department of Education, Vocational Education Division. If you call Advocacy Press, (805) 962-2728, we'd be glad to give you the name and address of the person in your state. Many *Choices/Challenges* programs receive funding from this source.

ORIENTATION AND COUNSELING

Choices and *Challenges* can be incorporated into student counseling programs at both the high school and college levels, either in a group setting or as independent study. The curriculum is particularly valuable for the way it stresses the importance of goal setting and then lays out and clarifies goal-setting techniques. This skill will serve students well in planning their school program and also throughout their lives.

PREGNANT TEEN/PARENTING PROGRAMS

Because *Choices* and *Challenges* help pregnant teens and young parents project themselves into the future and accept responsibility for their own lives, they are useful both for keeping these students in school and for avoiding a second pregnancy. The budget section is an eye-opener for those who have not considered the financial responsibilities of parenthood. The books also motivate these students to plan for training in a job that will allow them to be economically self-sufficient, and then show them how to go about getting the necessary education or training.

TEEN PREGNANCY PREVENTION

Young women who can project themselves into the future and visualize the kind of life they hope to lead are much less likely to become pregnant than those teens who are not so aware. *Choices* promotes self-awareness, assertiveness and goal setting, and emphasizes the need for further education in order to achieve economic self-sufficiency. It demonstrates the limitations imposed by early pregnancy, and encourages young women to set goals for achievement that will ultimately make family life a more rewarding experience.

Instructor's Notes:

Instructor's Notes:

Instructor's Notes:

Changes:

A Woman's Journal for
Self-awareness and Personal Planning

Mindy Bingham, Sandy Stryker and Judy Edmondson

Changes Curriculum

Introduction to Changes

When we first learned that adult women were buying *Choices* for themselves, we were surprised. Didn't they already know the basic skills it teaches? It soon became obvious that many of them did not. We heard that friends were buying *Choices* for their friends, daughters were buying it for their mothers, counselors were using it with their adult clients, and so on. When we implemented the *Mother-Daughter Choices Project*, which was primarily designed to help the daughters, we noted that adult women of all ages could benefit from a book of this kind.

As we examined *Choices* with an eye toward helping adult women, we saw that Chapter Seven, "What about Marriage and Children?" did not apply. While adult women were already aware of the issues surrounding parenthood, many were struggling with an entirely different problem-the problem of change.

Since change is almost as certain as death and taxes these days, being able to face it, accept it, or even go after it is an essential skill. If you don't believe that, consider how your own life has changed in the last five or ten years. What technological wonders-once thought exotic-do you now take for granted? Computers in the classroom? Microwave ovens? Cordless phones? VCRs and compact disc players? While all these gadgets are symptomatic of a society in rapid change, they are relatively easy to accept. It's the changes that disrupt our accustomed way of living that cause the most difficulty: marriage, divorce, illness, career change, birth of a child, children leaving home, retirement, aging, and so on.

While change is inevitable, it can be approached in different ways-with fear and regret, or with anticipation and excitement. We feel that the latter approach is most conducive to growth and life satisfaction. And so we began work on

Changes, a book that parallels *Choices* in Chapters One to Six and Eight to Twelve, but substitutes a chapter on change for *Choices*' Chapter Seven.

Although the examples in the two books differ, the exercises are the same. Consult pp. 17 to 110 in this guide for teaching suggestions and adapt them to your population. Guidance on the new Chapter Seven follows. (We've also included some additional suggestions for the Budget Exercise in Chapter Three.)

Because Changes parallels Choices, the two books can also be easily used in a Mother-Daughter Choices Project. Detailed information on this kind of project begins on p. 138.

See pp. 17 to 110 in this guide for curriculum ideas for *Changes'* Chapters One to Six and Eight to Twelve.

Additional Suggestions for Chapter Three

Many adult women are shockingly unaware of their families' personal finances. As countless widows and divorced women will testify, women pay the price for their ignorance by living in reduced circumstances or outright poverty when their husbands are no longer present.

Some suggestions:

Try to make the Budget Exercise as personal and as detailed as possible. Have participants determine how much their current lifestyle costs, what kind of savings or investments they have, what kind of insurance, and so on. Ask students to research and keep a log of names, addresses and account numbers for savings accounts, insurance policies, mortgage holders, and so on.

Women who own their own homes might investigate not only who holds the mortgage and their account number, but how much they currently owe, how many more years the mortgage has to run, the interest rate they are paying, and their monthly payment. How much are their property taxes? When are they due? How much insurance do they have on their home? What are the payments and when are they due? What is the current market value of the house? (They might need to contact a real estate agent for this figure.) Would it be a good idea to refinance the house? Shop around for a new insurance company?

What other kinds of insurance do these women have? Life insurance? Auto? Health? What companies hold each policy, what is the policy number, the coverage and the annual premium? When is it due?

Where are their savings accounts? What are the account numbers? How much have they saved? What interest rates are the accounts earning?

Ask participants to use receipts or their checkbook register (if they have one) to find figures on utility payments, groceries, car payments, or credit card payments for the past six months. Have them add the figures in each category and divide by six to get the average monthly expense.

Be sure participants note when large payments are due (taxes, insurance, mortgage, and so on) so they can budget accordingly.

Discuss possible ways to save money, such as using coupons or pumping their own gas.

Chapter Seven
Reacting to Change

PAGES 152-154 **Workbook 76**

Objective:

To help students analyze how they most often react to changes in their lives.

Presentation Suggestions:

Ask students to choose the answers that most closely match their own feelings about change. Follow with group discussion. How many women chose mostly "a" statements? Mostly "b"? Mostly "c"? Mostly "d"? In addition to improving students' self-knowledge, this exercise should give you an indication of the task at hand. If the class already has a favorable attitude toward change, you can proceed boldly. If a significant number of students are reluctant to accept change you will need to take a different tack, perhaps encouraging students to begin dealing with change at its least threatening level-changing a hairstyle or rearranging the furniture, for example.

Activities:

Ask students to think of events from the recent past in their own lives in which they reacted to change in each of the modes described. For example, a woman might be:

Enthusiastic about the birth of a child (mode *a*)

Excited but cautious about buying a new house (mode *b*)

Uneasy about changing jobs (mode *c*)

Fearful of getting divorced (mode *d*)

Follow with group discussion. Can students fit any patterns or hints about their mind-set in their answers? For example, did they find it easier to take physical risks? Emotional risks? Financial risks?

Ask students how the changes they listed above turned out. Were they right to be enthusiastic? Right to be afraid? If they had these decisions to make over again, would they approach them in the same way? If not, how would their approach differ?

Resources:

Friedman, Sonya. *Smart Cookies Don't Crumble*. New York: Pocket Books, 1985.

Naisbitt, John, and Patricia Aburdene. *Re-inventing the Corporation.* New York: Warner Books, 1985.

James, Jennifer. *Women and the Blues*. New York: Harper & Row, 1988.

Long-and Short-Term Changes

PAGE 155 **Workbook 77**

Objective:

To help students recognize the difference between short-term changes and long-term changes, what their consequences are, and how they differ.

Presentation Suggestions:

As a class, think of as many short-term and long-term changes as you can. Then go back and ask students to determine the consequences of each change, assuming they determine it was an undesirable one. The class should see that, in general, short-term changes have less serious consequences than long-term changes. For example, it's much easier to go back to your old hairstyle than it is to get out of an unhappy marriage. Recognizing "the worst that could happen" in any situation often leads to wiser decisions.

Activities:

Invite people who have made various kinds of changes successfully to discuss what they changed, why and how. Form a panel, or have a series of individuals come in throughout the time you are working on this chapter. You might include people who have had to change because of illness or accident, people who have moved to the United States from another country, people who have suddenly made or lost a great deal of money, people who have moved from the city to the country as well as people who have changed careers, appearance, or marital status.

Changing Values and Economic Necessity

PAGES 156-159 Workbook 78-79

Objective:

To help students evaluate whether the change they need/want to make has come about because of changing values and/or economic necessity. If the change is necessitated by economics alone, students may need to reframe their goals to keep them in line with their values.

Presentation Suggestions:

Have students complete the exercise individually, and follow with group discussion. Pay special attention to those women forced to change through economic necessity. Perhaps the class can help them rephrase their goals so that the required change will still reflect their old values. (See Emily's example in the book.)

Resources:

Naisbitt, John. *Megatrends*. New York: Warner Books, 1984.

Getting Support for Change

PAGE 160 Workbook 78-79

Objective:

To point out to students that they will need positive support in order to make major life changes, and to help them evaluate or identify where they can hope to find that support.

Presentation Suggestions:

Have students complete the exercise individually. Be prepared to offer suggestions if students cannot think of likely sources of support.

Activities:

Invite a counselor, therapist or member of the clergy familiar with the process of change to speak to the class and answer questions.

Physical and Emotional Energy

PAGE 161 **Workbook 80**

Objective:

To help students evaluate whether they currently have the physical and emotional energy to make a change, or whether the change should be postponed (assuming it can be postponed).

Presentation Suggestions:

We often overlook the fact that change — even desirable change — requires energy and causes stress. Ask the students to evaluate their own situation by choosing the answers that best reflect their current physical and mental state. Those who answer "c" to a majority of the questions should be encouraged to postpone their change, if they can. Instead, they need to concentrate on gaining confidence and regaining health. Then they will be in a better position to proceed. Encourage any students with a majority of "c" answers, who are being forced to change immediately, to pay particular attention to their health and to surround themselves with as much support as they can.

Action Plan for Change

PAGES 162-165 **Workbook 81-84**

Objective:

To have students use all the skills they have developed thus far — goal setting, values clarification, assertiveness — to set up an action plan for making a successful change.

Presentation Suggestions:

If necessary, review the sections of the book on values and skills identification, goal setting and decision making. Then have students complete their action plan. Remind them that this model can be used for any change they want, or need, to make throughout their lives.

Follow-Up:

Have students once again take the Attitudes Quiz at the beginning of the chapter. Do they feel more comfortable with the idea of change?

Take a copy of each student's action plan and agree to mail it to them at a specified time. (Ask the class decide when-three months from today? A year?) This will serve as a reminder for students who have lost sight of their goal, while bolstering the self-confidence of those who have completed their plan.

> **NOTE:** If the women in your *Changes* program are of child-bearing age, they will also benefit from information in *More Choices: A Strategic Planning Guide for Mixing Career and Family.* To order a copy write to Advocacy Press, P.O. Box 236, Santa Barbara, CA 93102. (805) 962-2728.

Changes:
A Woman's Journal for
Self-awareness and Personal Planning
Mindy Bingham, Sandy Stryker and Judy Edmondson

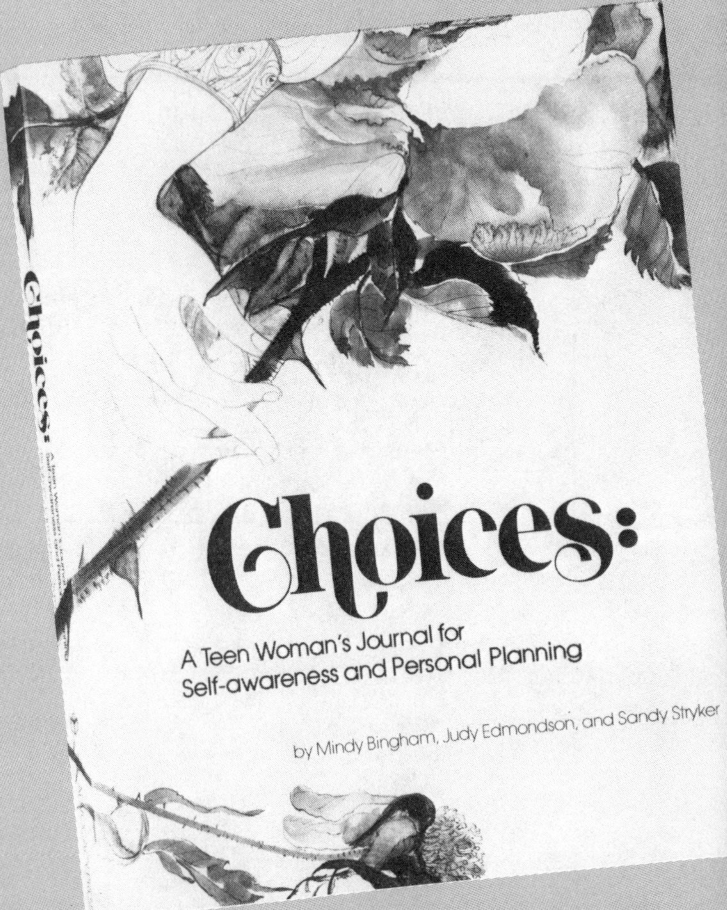
Choices:
A Teen Woman's Journal for
Self-awareness and Personal Planning
by Mindy Bingham, Judy Edmondson, and Sandy Stryker

Mother/Daughter Curriculum

Goals of the program include:

- Promoting mother-daughter communication.
- Providing a framework in which mothers and daughters can share their love and support for one another.
- Developing a support network between girls, between women, and among all the girls and women in the group.
- Clarifying the need for girls to examine their attitudes about their futures and their expectations of the working world.
- Motivating girls to expand their vision of themselves and of their capabilities.
- Improving self-esteem and self-confidence.
- Promoting assertive and responsible behavior.
- Teaching valuable life skills including problem solving, decision making, goal planning.
- Helping to build girls' capacities to become economically independent.
- Offering women the opportunity to assess and evaluate their own career options and life choices.
- Getting people acquainted and involved.
- Having fun in the process!

Curriculum for Mother-Daughter Choices Project

The *Mother-Daughter Choices Project*, a special program for sixth-grade or pre-teen girls and their mothers, is designed to prepare young girls for the kinds of decisions they will be making as they move into junior high school, high school and beyond. The transition into junior high school has long been recognized as a critical time in the lives of young people; it demands skills in problem solving, decision making and goal setting. It's also a time when peer pressure begins to exert considerable influence, and when communication with parents begins to falter.

The *Mother-Daughter Choices Project* provides the opportunity for mothers and daughters to communicate, in a relaxed, supportive atmosphere, about some of the issues that concern them. It encourages the development of a support network between the mothers and daughters participating in the groups, at the same time that it teaches valuable life skills. Some additional goals include: clarifying the need for girls to examine their attitudes about their futures and their expectations about the working world, motivating girls to expand their visions of themselves and of their capabilities, improving self-esteem and self-confidence, promoting assertive and responsible behavior.

As its name indicates, the Mother-*Daughter Choices Project* is also for mothers. They, too, will benefit from the information and insights to be gained by participating in the groups. As workers or homemakers and parents, mothers lead stressful and demanding lives. Part of the challenge for most women is to find the time, energy and resources to adapt to the many changes they face. It's not easy to juggle all the roles and responsibilities in our busy lives, and still stay in touch with our own very special goals and dreams. The *Mother-Daughter Choices Project* offers mothers of all ages the opportunity to rediscover these dreams, and to share with other women some of the best ways of achieving them. In the process, they'll learn or relearn skills such as setting a goal, solving a problem, and making a decision.

The program consists of six two-hour meetings, which are held one evening a week for six weeks in the homes of the participants. An initial planning meeting, for mothers only, precedes the six meetings, and a recreational activity selected by the group wraps them up. Each group of mothers and daughters has its own coordinator, and that individual will recruit the mother of a fifth-grade girl to coordinate a group for the following year. In this way, the *Mother-Daughter Choices Project* is self-perpetuating. Getting people acquainted and involved, and providing a framework for mothers and daughters to share their hopes and dreams for the future, as well as their love and support for one another, is what this program is all about.

The curriculum for the Mother-Daughter *Choices* Project is taken from selected material covered in the first six chapters of *Choices* and *Changes*. Although some of the exercises may be too advanced for the sixth grader, many of them are not. The advantage of *Choices* is that it is a flexible format, which can be modified for use by children, teens or adults. The sixth-grade or pre-teen girl will be able to use and understand more of *Choices* as she develops and matures. The book becomes a part of the process of growing up and becoming aware of the real world and options for the future.

For mothers, there is a companion book entitled *Changes*. *Changes* has been written specifically for the adult woman who is interested in discovering her own options for the future. It follows a workbook-style format with activities paralleling those in *Choices*, enabling mothers and daughters to do the exercises together, each in her own book. By joining their daughters in this kind of exploration, mothers serve as role models. Several studies have proven that parents' attitudes have significant impact on childrens' choices of occupation and levels of achievement. In fact, parental influences are the best predictors of girls' achievement in careers that are non-traditional.

NOTE: Variations of the *Mother-Daughter CHOICES Project* exist. Call Advocacy Press for information on the Father-Daughter, Mother-Son, and Father-Son versions of the *Project*.

Questions Commonly Asked about the Mother-Daughter Choices Project

Why was the sixth-grade or pre-teen girl chosen as the candidate for this program?

The sixth grade is recognized as a critical transition stage. It is at the threshold of junior high school, a time when peer pressure accelerates, and yet it is an age when parental opinion and authority are still respected. Life skills such as decision making, assertiveness and goal setting are important for girls, especially, to acquire at a young age. Girls will be making decisions in junior high that have long-term effects on both their academic and personal goals. Deciding not to take math and science courses, for example, will hinder their chances for economic success. Other decisions concerning drug or alcohol usage and sexuality confront girls at earlier ages; the Mother-Daughter Choices Project provides the basis for acquiring the skills that will enable them to take charge of their lives.

Would this program work with girls from grades seven through twelve?

Yes, it can work for older girls. However, peer pressure is most influential during the teen years and some adolescent girls would not want to be seen in the same room with their mothers. This developmental issue needs to be considered when forming a group of mothers and older daughters. Part of a teenager's maturation process is to individuate from parents and family. This is normal and desirable, even if it is often painful and frustrating to both parents and teens. It is best to establish communication skills and rapport BEFORE the teen years.

What about groups of girls below the sixth grade?

This program is not recommended for girls younger than the sixth-grade level. Most fifth and fourth graders are not developmentally ready to tackle the program content; it is often far too difficult for them.

What about groups made up of girls from different age groups?

Because of the stated goal of building support networks among peers, the program works better if the girls come from a similar age group such as a neighborhood, athletic team, or church group. It is best to try to stay within one, perhaps two, grade levels. Girls are changing rapidly at this age, and each year brings new interests and concerns. Because group discussion is such a central component of the program, it is important that girls have a common frame of reference. This usually means they will be about the same age.

What are the characteristics of a group that works well?

We recommend putting together a group that is a natural peer group, a group that will continue to benefit from the open communication and support, once the activity has ended. The most obvious is a group of classmates and their mothers. Or you can look to other on-going groups such as church groups, scouts, athletic teams, 4-H, YWCAs, and the like.

One of the strengths of this program is the development of support networks between the girls and their mothers. This support is important to girls during the teen years. Try to put together a group that will have the opportunity to continue that support.

What is the ideal size of a group?

Between four and eight mother-daughter pairs seem to be the ideal size (eight to sixteen participants).

What about the girl without a mother able to participate?

It is important to identify those girls in your daughter's group who may not have mothers to participate with them. There are any number of reasons why this could be the case. Often there is no mother in the home or the mother is unable or unwilling to join the group. Try to find this out BEFORE YOU BEGIN RECRUITING mother-daughter pairs. If you are recruiting from your daughter's class, visit her teachers ahead of time and ask if they are aware of any such situation. If you are recruiting from another group, ask the same question of the person most familiar with the personal lives of the participants: i.e., youth leader, scout leader, coach, or minister.

If you identify a girl with a special need, it would be wise to contact the mother or guardian of that child directly (before you pass out the flyer to the girls), to explain the program and see if you can arrange for the girl to participate even if her mother cannot. Another female figure: an aunt, grandmother, or a trusted friend can complete the project with the sixth grader.

Here is where adult mentors might be useful. Local women's organizations or youth serving organizations might have an individual who will participate as a partner to a girl who would like to experience the project. Let the girls you are asking know that there are adults would like to work with them.

Why was the program designed to last six weeks?

For many families today, a six-week commitment is about as long as anyone can make. That is one reason why a program like this is so needed; family members are often too busy to spend precious time together. This program gives them an opportunity to do so at a time when their daughters most need it.

What seems to be the ideal length of each meeting?

Each meeting has been designed to take two hours. If your group is going to deviate from this time frame, you will need to adjust your expectations concerning what you can accomplish each time.

What is a good setting for the meetings?

Because of the intimate nature of the discussions, it is important that the group have a private meeting area that is free of interruptions from others, so that participants may be assured that no outsiders are listening.

Most groups choose to rotate the six meetings among the homes of the participants. A living room is comfortable and lends itself to the congenial feeling of the activity. Often, other family members spend the evening doing another activity away from home.

Is it necessary for each mother to have a copy of *Changes* and each daughter to have a copy of *Choices?*

Although the ideal situation is for each mother and daughter to have her own copy, economics may preclude this. Many of the meetings can be conducted verbally.

May fathers or other male adults join the groups?

We recommend that fathers or other men use the book *Challenges*, available from Advocacy Press. Both fathers and sons would use the book, *Challenges*; mother-son groups would use *Changes* and *Challenges*. Most groups/meetings are conducted with members all of the same sex. For many teenaged girls, privacy is an important issue. The presence of men or boys can inhibit what the girls might say. With a little adjustment here and there, the program may be used in various ways in other settings. It is good to include men in the groups as guest speakers in order to get a male perspective; they certainly have a good deal to contribute, and we welcome their participation.

Job Description of the Mother-Daughter Coordinator

The Mother-Daughter coordinator can be either a parent of one of the girls in the group or an interested third party who will act as the facilitator for the group. The coordinator needs to be highly interested in the processes and willing to devote the time to organize, recruit and prepare for the weekly meetings.

Promotion and Recruitment

1. Order videotape (if desired) and one copy each of *Choices* and *Changes* to begin promoting the program. Many libraries also have these books available.
2. Decide on the group of girls that will be invited to join the Mother-Daughter Project. An example would be your daughter's female sixth-grade classmates.
3. Visit that group's leader (e.g., the teacher) to explain the program and inquire if there are any girls who might have difficulty participating because they have no mother available.
4. Contact the above-mentioned families and try to help them work something out before you begin general recruiting.
5. Send out flyers and invitations to the Mothers' meeting to all the mothers of the girls in your daughter's group.
6. Hold the Mothers' Meeting.
7. Mail out copies of the meeting schedule to each participating mother.
8. Order books if the group decides to use them.

Meetings' Facilitation

1. Each week study the agenda carefully ahead of time and come prepared to facilitate the group.
2. Share the duty of facilitator with other mother(s) in the group, if you wish. You can decide who is responsible for which night's activity.
3. You are responsible for calling the meeting to order each time and making sure the group is productive and everyone is involved. You are the official facilitator and the parliamentarian of the group's process.
4. Recruit one or two mothers to be involved with the planning and execution of the group's recreational activity after the sixth meeting.

Follow Up

The Mother-Daughter coordinator is responsible for recruiting and introducing a new coordinator to the Mother-Daughter Choices Project. In the case of the group of classmates, this would be the mother of a current fifth-grade girl. In other cases, it would be an individual (mother of a sixth grader or not) who wants to find out about coordinating a group of sixth-grade girls and their mothers. You may also recruit the mother of another sixth grader so that more girls and their mothers may enjoy the program. However, to make the program truly self-perpetuating for a succession of sixth-grade girls, you will want to recruit another sixth grader's mother only after recruiting a fifth-grader's mother. Invite whomever you select to observe one or two or your later sessions. This is often enough to convince someone to take on the leadership role for a subsequent group.

A Sample Calendar of Events

8 WEEKS BEFORE THE FIRST GROUP MEETING

- ☐ Your *Mother-Daughter Handbook* arrives in the mail.
- ☐ Read through it and decide how you want to proceed.
- ☐ Order the video tape if you plan to use it.

7 WEEKS BEFORE THE FIRST GROUP MEETING

- ☐ Decide on which girls and mothers you want to invite to join the group.
- ☐ Decide on the day, time and location of the Mothers' Meeting.
- ☐ Visit with the leader of any existing group you may have selected to identify any special needs of any of the girls within that group. An example would be a girl without a mother able to participate.
- ☐ If you do identify such a girl, call that parent or guardian to explain the program and make suggestions on how that girl might still be involved.
- ☐ Recruit a co-coordinator if you would like to share the leadership of the meetings.

6 WEEKS BEFORE THE FIRST GROUP MEETING

- ☐ Photocopy and send invitations and flyers to each of the mothers and daughters within your daughter's group (classroom, church group or whatever you have chosen as a peer group).
- ☐ Wait for RSVPs.
- ☐ Place follow-up calls to mothers to finalize meeting time and date.

4 WEEKS BEFORE THE FIRST GROUP MEETING

- ☐ Hold the Mothers' Meeting. Describe the program and get commitments to participate.
- ☐ At Mothers' Meeting establish calendar of meeting dates, times and locations and mail to each mother.
- ☐ Order books if the group has decided to use them. Allow three to four weeks for delivery. You can shorten this by adding $1.00 per book for parcel post mailing.

4 WEEKS LATER BEGIN WITH THE FIRST MOTHER-DAUGHTER MEETING

- ☐ See detailed week-by-week agenda beginning on p. 147 in the *Mother-Daughter Choices Handbook.*

BEFORE THE LAST OF THE SIX SESSIONS

- ☐ Identify a Mother-Daughter Choices coordinator who can lead a group next time. If you are working through the schools, this would mean finding the mother of a current fifth grader. If you are working through another group, it means finding a person interested in coordinating another Mother-Daughter *Choices* group. Invite the individual you have identified to attend one of your last sessions as an observer. Remember, the coordinator does not have to be a mother of a sixth grader or a daughter. This is one way of conducting the program, but there are many others as well. The coordinator need only be interested in working with sixth-grade girls and their mothers.
- ☐ Decide as a group on the recreational activity and decide on the logistics of the activity.

Coordinator Handbook Available

A complete guide is available to anyone wishing to start a *Mother-Daughter Choices Project.* It includes recruitment ideas, invitations, schedules, outlines of the meetings and graduation certificates. Also a two-hour training video tape is available which demonstrates how to present the material. Contact Advocacy Press, P.O. Box 236, Santa Barbara, CA, (805) 962-2728 for further details.

In Preparation for Each Session

TIMING

Before you begin each session, read the exercises and presentation suggestions. Rough out your own time schedule so you can glance at it during the session to see if you are on target. A sample agenda has been provided for each meeting.

Agenda for the Mothers' Meeting

Task	Minutes
Introductions by pairs	10
Take Startling Statement Quiz, correct and discuss	20
Video or presentation	20
Discussion	15
Finalize calendar	20
Decide on books	10
Decide on each person's task	15
Discuss special child-care needs	10

Some General Guidelines for the Curriculum

One of your key roles as coordinator is to keep the group moving and on target when appropriate, yet, at the same time, to be sensitive to the needs of the group. You will need to be directive on the one hand and flexible on the other.

1. You do not have to follow the curriculum exactly as given. You may decide, because of limited time or other considerations, not to do some of it. This is fine. The curriculum is only a guideline.
2. If it is not working, if people are tired or seem uninspired by what they are doing, go on to another activity. Or, you could discuss how they feel. Is the activity too hard? Does it take too long? Ask their opinions.
3. Sometimes the meeting will take on a life of its own as a discussion becomes more interesting and prolonged. If participants are still eager to talk about something, do not move on to the next activity. It is okay, if everything is not done. The idea is to communicate and have fun together.
4. Please note that at times the texts will differ slightly in *Choices* and *Changes*. This is because issues and examples presented are age-appropriate. We suggest using the text in *Choices* in these instances. Mothers may wish to complete the exercises in their books at home and are encouraged to do so.

Ground Rules for the Group

5 Minutes

After the interview warm-up, group ground rules should be established. It is helpful to place a small sign near the group during the meeting with the suggested rules below:

1. Each person is entitled to her or his opinion.
2. All discussions should be confidential.
3. No "non-verbal" put downs. Example: rolling of eyes or shaking head.
4. Everyone can use the magic word, "pass," if they do not wish to answer a question.

Resource:

Caron, Ann F. *Don't Stop Loving Me: A Reassuring Guide for Mothers of Adolescent Daughters*. New York: Henry Holt & Co., 1991.

Group Warm-up

One of the main goals of the *Mother-Daughter Choices Project* is to build support networks between the daughter peer-group, the mother peer-group and between all the women and girls within the group.

In each session, the first activity is the group warm-up. It is an interview situation in which the women and girls form pairs, sometimes in mother-daughter pairs and sometimes not.

At the beginning of each session, two questions are presented to the group, one question for the girls to ask the women they are paired with, and one question for the women to ask the girls. If you have a pad and easel or a chalk board available, you will want to write down each question. The curriculum for each session gives you the suggested questions and instructions for group pairings.

Once the group is divided, ask each pair to interview one another for a total of five minutes. Then reassemble the group and have the pairs introduce each other, giving the answers to the questions asked. Reporting will take from 10 to 15 minutes.

These interviews are among the most popular features of the meetings. Not only do they help the girls realize that their mothers were young once too and probably experienced many of the things they will, but they also help the girls to realize that the women in the group may be a good source of information and guidance in the years ahead. Additionally, these interviews get the group talking and discussing at the very start of each no session and serve to warm them up for the time remaining.

After about the third week, you might suggest the girls bring in their own questions. Many sixth graders really enjoy this and may come in with long lists of questions not only for their own mothers, but also for the other women in the group. Some of the girl-generated questions have included:

"Tell us about your first kiss."

"What was your first date like?"

"What would you do differently if you had your life to live over?"

Often the questions the girls come up with have to do with dating, boys and relationships. Studies show that girls who can talk openly with their mothers about these issues are far less likely to become teen mothers. If questions that are sexually explicit come up in your group, you may wish to invite a guest speaker expert in sexuality education to one of your meetings. Planned Parenthood and other such organizations are excellent resources in this regard. We recommend the first interview-question pairing (at the first meeting) be between mother-daughter pairs. After the first week, girls should be paired with women other than their own mothers. For many girls it is less threatening to answer these questions with someone other than their own mother. You may hear giggles, gasps and, "I didn't know that!" as girls listen to the answers their mothers give.

Sample Agenda for the First Meeting

Group Warm-up	20 minutes
Group Ground Rules	5 minutes
Envision Your Life	20 minutes
Attitude Inventory	30 minutes
Bridge the Generation Gap	25 minutes
Group Wrap-up	announcements for next week

DIVIDE THE GROUP — Pair mothers with their own daughters.

Have the mothers interview the daughters with the question:

"What do you want to be when you grow up and why?"

Have the daughters interview their mothers with these questions:

"When you were my age, what did you want to be when you grew up? If you are not that today, why not?"

Sample Agenda for the Second Meeting

Group Warm-up	20 minutes
The Working World Exercise	40 minutes
Women in the Workforce Quiz	15 minutes
True Stories Activity	30 minutes
Selecting a Recreational Activity	15 minutes

DIVIDE THE GROUP — Put the names of the adults in the group in a hat. Ask each girl to draw a name out of the hat and pair up for the warm-up with this woman.

Have the adults ask the girls:

"If you could wave a magic wand and have your dream job, what would that be and why?"

Have the girls ask the adults:

"If you could go back in time to my age and change something about your life, what would it be?"

Sample Agenda for the Third Meeting

Group Warm-up	15 minutes
The Budget Exercise	1 hour 30 minutes
Finalize Recreational Activity	

NOTE: Chapter Three is time-consuming. Some groups take two weeks (two meetings) to complete it. Try to keep your group "on task" for this one.

Ask the girls to pair with adults they have not worked with yet. The questions for the girls to ask the women are:

"When you were growing up what did the following cost:

A hamburger?

A movie?

A house?

"Did you have an allowance? If so, what was it?"

The interview question for the women to ask the girls is:

"If you were an adult now and you got a job tomorrow, what would it be and how much money per year do you think you'd earn?"

Sample Agenda for the Fourth Meeting

Group Warm-up	15 minutes
Reporting out on Personal Budgets	10 minutes
Values Survey	45 minutes
Quiz: Applying Value Categories	25 minutes
Personal Values and Career Choice	20 minutes

Sample Agenda for the Fifth Meeting

Group Warm-up	15 minutes
Goal Setting Text and Explanation	15 minutes
Set Your Own Goals Exercise	15 minutes
The Action Plan	30 minutes
Decision Making	30 minutes
What Can You Do?	15 minutes

Sample Agenda for the Sixth Meeting

Group Warm-up	15 minutes
Assertiveness	20 minutes
Assertive, Aggressive, Passive	15 minutes
Write Your Own Responses	20 minutes
Sharing Experiences & Truth and Consequence	15 minutes
OPTIONAL — What Causes Unplanned Pregnancies?	25 minutes
Wrap-up and Planning for Recreational Activity	10 minutes

NOTE: It is quite helpful to the staff at Advocacy Press if the evaluation forms at the end of the *Handbook for the Coordinator* are filled out anonymously by group participants. If a coordinator returns the evaluations, he or she receives a $10.00 gift certificate good towards the purchase of any Advocacy Press publication.

More Choices:
A Strategic Planning Guide for Mixing Career and Family
by Mindy Bingham and Sandy Stryker

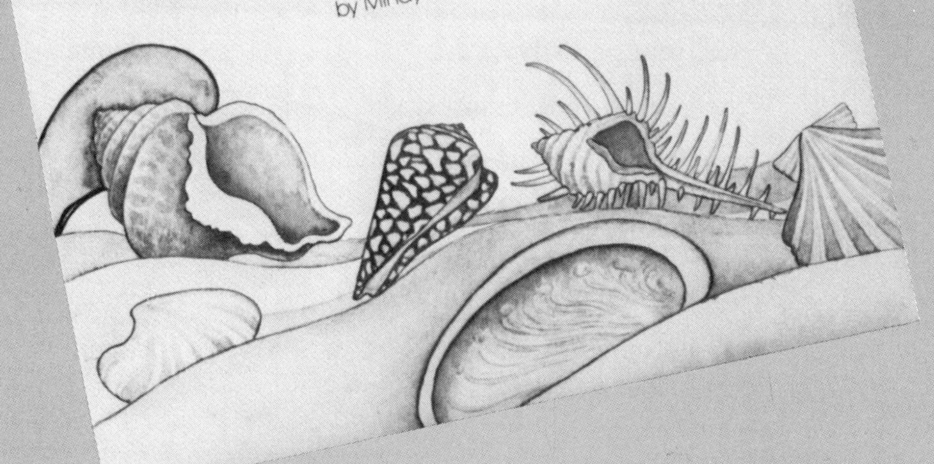

More Choices Curriculum

More Choices Introduction

Our reason for writing *More Choices* was brought home, not for the first time, by a news article examining the life of a young, single mother struggling to complete her education. Like all of us, this woman had choices to make. "Often," she said, "the choice was whether to buy food for her family or diapers for her baby." Clearly, choices like this are unacceptable. Yet, every day, more American women are finding themselves in a similar predicament.

And it's not entirely their fault. They did what they were expected to do — marry, have babies, and sit back to wait for a fairy tale ending that somehow eludes most of them. Women who want to have a family and most of them do — often do not realize the importance of an education, or the likelihood that they may need to support themselves and their children at some time in their lives.

Statistics show that six million American women are the sole support of families with children under the age of 18-thirteen percent of all white families, 44 percent of all black families and 23 percent of all Hispanic families. Over one-third of these families live in poverty.

Married women, half of whom have children under the age of six, are also likely to work outside the home. Two-thirds of all women between the ages of 25 and 55 are in the workforce. Most, however, work at "traditional" women's jobs, that generally do not pay well enough to support a family.

Millions of American families, too, are struggling with the multifaceted problems involved in juggling career, family and personal responsibilities.

Career education courses have been largely unsuccessful at convincing young women that they need to consider future work outside the home at least as seriously as the young men in these classes do. And young men still tend to believe that their wives will handle the majority of household and child-care tasks. At this time they are right, but most working women would agree that these tasks need to be shared more equitably.

More Choices attempts to remedy both problems. As far as we know, it is the only text that combines career and life planning and illustrates how decisions made in one sphere of life will inevitably have an impact on the other. It encourages young women to prepare seriously for a career by showing how the right job can give them more options and improve their family life. It forces young men to explore their feelings about child care, housework, self-health and the benefits of leading a balanced life.

Feminine names are used in most of the stories and examples throughout the book, but *More Choices* is by no means meant to be used solely by young women. The book is written as it is because women's lives have changed so drastically in recent years that their need for *More Choices* is extreme. Though the male consciousness still lags behind, sooner or later men, too, must adjust to this changing world. Using the book in a co-educational setting is likely to promote lively discussions and serve as an eye opener for students of both sexes.

Ideally, students — especially younger teens — should work through the pre-career awareness exercises in *Choices* or *Challenges* before approaching the more advanced life-planning information in *More Choices*. Older students, or those who have had other instruction in the topics of *Choices* and *Challenges,* may be ready for *More Choices*. You are in the best position to make this decision.

The book can be used with various populations, and in many settings, including home economics classes, career development/life planning programs, single mother/teen-parent programs, vocational readiness programs, displaced homemaker programs, parenting/family life programs and drop-out prevention programs. You will find more detailed information on how to use the book in these settings at the end of this section, beginning on p. 233.

Chapter One

The first chapter of *More Choices* is meant to make students aware of some of the more common myths concerning the lives of girls and women. It suggests some possible sources for these myths and asks students to consider whether they contain any truth. As students begin to question the validity of the myths, they may have to rethink some of their assumptions about their own lives. This is the first step in creating the realization among students that they are *not* likely to have a fairy tale existence, but that they can take positive steps to have the kind of life they will find most satisfying.

Myth # 2
It's Only a Story

PAGES 14-15 **Workbook 4**

Objective:

To help students recognize some of the messages presented-overtly or covertly-by the stories they are likely to have heard repeated many times during their childhood.

Presentation Suggestions:

Ask students to draw lines connecting each of the stories with the messages they convey. There may be more than one answer for each message and/or story. They include the following:

Some day my prince will come: *Cinderella, Snow White, Rapunzel, Sleeping Beauty, Beauty and the Beast*

And they lived happily ever after: *Cinderella, Snow White, Rapunzel, Sleeping Beauty*

Women are vain and jealous: *Cinderella, Snow White, Rapunzel, Sleeping Beauty, Hansel and Gretel*

Step-parents are evil: *Cinderella, Snow White, Hansel and Gretel*

Women belong in castles and towers: *Cinderella, Snow White, Rapunzel, Sleeping Beauty*

Men belong on thrones or horses: *Cinderella, Snow White, Rapunzel, Sleeping Beauty, Beauty and the Beast*

Women get what they want through magic, scheming, or being "nice": *Cinderella, Snow White, Rapunzel, Sleeping Beauty, Beauty and the Beast*

Men get what they want through work and bravery: *Cinderella, Snow White, Rapunzel, Sleeping Beauty, Hansel and Gretel, Beauty and the Beast*

Women must have long hair and small feet: *Cinderella, Rapunzel*

Women need to be rescued: *Cinderella, Snow White, Rapunzel, Sleeping Beauty, Hansel and Gretel, Beauty and the Beast*

Men are the rescuers: *Cinderella, Snow White, Rapunzel, Sleeping Beauty, Hansel and Gretel, Beauty and the Beast*

Women are self-sacrificing: *Cinderella, Snow White, Rapunzel, Sleeping Beauty*

Men go after what they want: *Cinderella, Snow White, Rapunzel, Sleeping Beauty, Hansel and Gretel, Beauty and the Beast*

It is dangerous for girls to have adventures: *Hansel and Gretel, Little Red Riding Hood, Goldilocks and the Three Bears*

Activities:

Statistics show that by age four children's perceptions and aspirations for adult occupations are sex-typed. The girls are likely to see fewer options for their lives than the boys. Ask students to consider whether any of the messages in the stories above might contribute to this fact. Ask them to consider favorite stories from their own childhood, especially ones not listed here. Also ask students in your class who might have been raised in a culture outside of the United States about the stories they remember. What messages did they get from those stories?

Ask students with younger brothers or sisters to bring in more recent children's books. Do they convey the same messages, or have they changed? Chances are, in addition to traditional stories, students will bring in books by Dr. Seuss, Maurice Sendak, Shel Silverstein, Beverly Cleary, or those featuring Sesame Street characters. These authors send new messages, but the old stories are still very much around. Do students think children today are getting better messages? Worse messages? The same messages? Mixed messages? Why?

You might want to read *Father Gander Nursery Rhymes: The Equal Rhymes Amendment* (Advocacy Press, 1985) aloud and compare these rhymes with those of the traditional Mother Goose.

Or, read *Minou* (Advocacy Press, 1987). Minou lived a *Cinderella* life. Her owner, Madame Violette, saw to her every need. Minou probably would have lived "happily ever after," but tragedy struck and Minou found herself on her own, completely unprepared to take care of herself. She learned the skills to become self-sufficient. The story introduces a life concept still, regrettably, missing from much of our children's literature: the reality that everyone, especially young women, must be prepared to care for themselves.

Ask students to write their own contemporary adaptations of familiar stories and fairy tales.

Resources:

Bingham, Mindy. *Minou.* Santa Barbara, CA: Advocacy Press, 1987.

Dowling, Colette. *The Cinderella Complex.* New York: Simon & Schuster, 1981.

Gander, Father. *Father Gander Nursery Rhymes: The Equal Rhymes Amendment.* Santa Barbara, CA: Advocacy Press, 1985.

Kolbenschlag, Madonna. *Kiss Sleeping Beauty Good-Bye.* New York: Bantam Books, 1979.

Pogrebin, Letty Cottin. *Stories for Free Children.* New York: McGraw Hill Book Company, 1982.

Sheehan, Patty, *Kylie's Song.* Santa Barbara, CA: Advocacy Press, 1988.

Sheehan, Patty, *Shadow and The Ready Time*, Santa Barbara, CA: Advocacy Press, 1994.

TV Trivia

PAGES 17-19 **Workbook 5-7**

Objective:

To analyze the messages delivered by popular TV shows of the past decades. How have they helped shape our ideas about acceptable roles for the sexes?

Presentation Suggestions:

Ask students to complete the quiz, startling at the point where most are familiar with the programs listed. Since these shows are heavily syndicated, age of students may not be a significant factor.

Ricky Ricardo is an entertainer; *Lucy* is a housewife.

Jim Anderson sells insurance; *Margaret* is a housewife.

Perry Mason is a lawyer; *Della Street* is an unmarried secretary.

Ward Cleaver is a professional; *June* is a housewife.

Miss Brooks is a single teacher who would like to be married.

The *main characters* in "How to Marry a Millionaire" are women determined to do just that.

Rob Petrie is a TV writer; *Laura* is a housewife. *Sally* is a single TV writer looking for a husband.

Dr. Kildare is a man.

The *main characters* in "Route 66" are men who travel around the country in a sports car to find adventure.

All the *single parents* in the '60s and most of the '70s are men.

Jim Kirk is captain of the Enterprise; *Mr. Spock* is a science officer; *Scotty* is chief engineer; *Bones* is a doctor; *Uhura* is communications officer. (Compare to the actors' roles in *Star Trek: The Next Generation.*)

Mary Richards is an associate producer; *Lou Grant*, the producer. She is single; he is married and has children.

Archie Bunker is a blue-collar worker; *Edith* is a housewife.

George Jefferson runs a chain of dry cleaning stores; *Louise* is a housewife.

Hawkeye and *B.J.* are doctors; *Margaret* is a nurse.

Lucy Bates is a single police officer; *Frank Furillo* is a married police captain with a child; *Joyce Davenport* is a childless, married lawyer.

The single parents in *Kate and Allie* are women.

Cliff Huxtable is a doctor; *Claire* is a lawyer. They are married and have children.

Steve Keaton works for public TV; *Elyse* is an architect who works at home. They are married and have children.

What messages do these TV shows send about the kinds of work men should do? Men are usually in positions of authority, make more money and have more adventures.

What messages do these TV shows send about the kinds of work women should do? Women are usually homemakers, or they work in subordinate positions requiring less education and paying less money. Or the "jobs" women do hold give the illusion of paying more than they do in the real world.

When men and women work together in these programs, who is usually the boss? The man is usually the boss.

If a woman works outside the home, is she more likely to be single or married? Working women are more likely to be single.

Do male TV characters often combine career, marriage and children? Yes.

How do female TV characters often combine career, marriage and children? Often they are expected to choose one among the three or seem to have some means of support not seen by the audience.

Are there many images of black, Asian, Hispanic or Native American women at home or at work? Until recently, almost none. Or, if represented, the characters act in stereotyped ways.

What changes do you see in the most recent TV shows? The most recent programs show women as workers and mothers, but may be in danger of perpetuating the Superwoman myth.

Students should become more aware of the need to be conscious of these media messages after completing this quiz. (See *Choices* for more exercises on the media.)

Resources:

"Killing Us Softly" and "Still Killing Us Softly," documentaries. See p. 24 of this guide.

Mason, Mary A. *The Equality Trap: Why Women Are in Trouble at Home & at Work.* New York: Simon & Schuster, Inc., 1988.

Myth # 3
Motherhood Is a Lifetime Job

PAGES 20-21 **Workbook 8**

Objective:

To help young women now planning to have family-centered lives to recognize that there will be many years to fill after their children are on their own.

Presentation Suggestions:

The thermometer diagram in the book represents a life span. Ask students to start at the **bottom** of the thermometer and draw a line from the questions to the corresponding age on the thermometer. After completing the statements, students should have a more realistic picture of the percentage of their lives in which parenting will not be a primary role.

Ask students to consider the lives of their own mothers and other adult women. How do they spend their time? Do any of them have jobs outside the home?

Activities:

Invite as a guest speaker someone who has raised a family and is now successfully pursuing a career or working as a volunteer.

Myth #4
I Can Be a Superwoman

PAGE 22 **Workbook 9**

Objective:

To help students determine whether their expectations to "have it all" and "do it all" are realistic.

Presentation Suggestions:

Ask students to consider the life of a woman they think of as a Superwoman and write her story. The person may be real or fictional. What is a typical day like for this woman? Where does she live? What kind of maintenance is necessary for her house or apartment? What kind of a family does she have? What are her hobbies? How much time does she devote to each activity? Have students add up the number of hours. Do they think that is a reasonable amount of time? Does it leave time for things like sleep? What things might this woman have to sacrifice to keep up her lifestyle?

Examples:

Fictional Superwomen:

Ann Kelsey on "LA Law"
Claire Huxtable on the "Bill Cosby Show"
Elyse Keaton on "Family Ties"
Murphy Brown on "Murphy Brown"

Celebrity Superwomen:

Connie Chung
Jane Pauley
Goldie Hawn
Candice Bergen
Felicia Rashad (Compare her real life to the one depicted on "The Cosby Show.")

Ask the male students: What would be the pros and cons of living with a Superwoman?

Activities:

Invite a panel of women who are attempting to mix career and family to share the joys, possibilities, limitations and frustrations of their lives.

Resources:

McLauglin, Steven D. *The Changing Lives of American Women.* Chapel Hill, North Carolina: University of North Carolina, 1988.

Instructor's Notes:

Chapter Two

After having some of their assumptions challenged in Chapter One, students are faced with some disturbing facts in Chapter Two. Reality steps in to take the place of myth. Together, Chapters One and Two create the proper mind-set for dealing with the material that follows. Students have increased awareness and understanding of the problems they are likely to face as workers and parents and will be more motivated to pursue workable solutions.

Which World Do You Live In?

PAGES 26-28 **Workbook 10-12**

Objective:

To have students analyze their own experiences and how they relate to the rest of society. This exercise sets the framework for the startling statement quizzes that follow by allowing students to compare the lives of people they know to those of the general population.

Presentation Suggestions:

Ask the students to list on the chart provide the names of people to whom they are close and then fill in the boxes with answers to the questions that follow. You might have the class pick one student as an example and write her/his chart on the board. After completing their charts, students are to use the information they have gathered to fill in the blanks of the "news release" that follows.

Since each student's sample consists of ten subjects, percentages can be figured by counting those who fit a particular category and multiplying by ten. If two families are headed by single parents, 20 percent of the families sampled fall into this category (2 x 10 = 20%).

Turn back to this chart after completing the startling statement quizzes and have students determine whether their lives are typical compared to the lives of other Americans today.

Realities #1 #2 and #3
Startling Statement Quizzes

PAGES 29-32 and PAGES 35-36 **Workbook 13-14, 17**

Objective:

To expose students to the truth about working women, child care, divorce and poverty in America today.

Presentation Suggestions:

Startling statement quizzes which present statistics that might otherwise be easily passed over and forgotten, have been found to be an effective way to make an impact on students. Students should complete each statement with the figures they feel are correct, and thus are forced to think about the issue and their own impressions of it. If they complete the statement correctly, their impressions are reinforced. If they get the answer wrong, the correct answer often makes a deep impression, one that will not be soon forgotten. Ask your students to complete one quiz at a time, and follow with group discussion.

Energizer:

An alternate plan is to divide the class into groups of three and have each group come to a consensus about the correct statistics. Offer a prize to the group getting the most answers correct. (Use a tie-breaker by using one of the questions from another quiz in the *CHOICES* series in the event of a tie.) The prize motivates students and encourages lively debate within each group as members work through the questions. Students will need to examine their own thoughts and where they came from, as well as to hear what their classmates perceive to be the truth. Again, follow up with a large group discussion.

You might use the class to illustrate some of the statistics. For example, you would ask every third student to stand. The standing students represent one-third of all families maintained by a woman living in poverty in this country.

Resources:

Hewlett, Sylvia Ann. *A Lesser Life: The Myth of Women's Liberation in America.* New York: William Morrow & Company, 1986.

Lenz, Elinor, and Barbara Myerhoff. *The Feminization of America: How Women's Values are Changing Our Public and Private Lives.* Los Angeles, CA: Jeremy P. Tarcher, Inc., 1985.

Facts and Reflections on Careers for Today's Girls. Girls Incorporated National Resource Center, 441 West Michigan Street, Indianapolis, IN 46202, 1985. (317)634-7546.

National Commission on Children, *Beyond Rhetoric, A New American Agenda for Children and Families.* U.S. Government Printing Office, Washington, D.C., 1991.

Film:

"Gentle Angry People," Catholic Charities USA, 1319 F Street, NW. Washingon D.C., 20004. (202) 639-8400.

Talk to a Single Mother/Father

PAGES 33-34 **Workbook 15-16**

Objective:

To compare the lives of single mothers and fathers and to promote awareness of the need for economic autonomy.

Presentation Suggestions:

Assign the interviews as homework and follow up with class discussion. If students have trouble finding a single father, you may want to invite one to class for a group interview. See p. 22 of this guide for interview techniques.

Follow-Up:

What problems are common to both single fathers and mothers?

If they are trying to raise children and work at the same time, they are probably suffering from a lack of time and flexibility in their lives.

What are the different problems?

Most often, women will have more economic problems; men have more trouble dealing with relationships and household tasks.

How might the women be better prepared?

They could have planned for a career that would make it easier to support themselves and their children.

How might the men be better prepared?

They might have learned how to care for children, cook, or do housework.

Did any of the parents say they *expected* to be raising their children alone?

Reality #4
Equal, but Different
A Society in Transition

PAGE 37 **Workbook 18-19**

Objective:

To review the chapter and reinforce its message: Mixing career and family is a difficult but often inescapable task that can be made easier with careful planning.

Presentation Suggestions:

Ask each student to write a short essay on one of the questions and report back to class. Discuss with the group.

Follow-Up:

Have students turn in answers to these questions now. At the end of the course, have them answer the same questions again to see how much their awareness has changed.

Instructor's Notes:

Chapter Three

Even more than politics and religion, money has been considered a taboo subject for consideration in polite society. Women, in particular, tend to feel that it is inappropriate for them to be concerned about finances. In an ideal world, it might not be necessary for anyone to worry about who is going to pay the bills. But this is not an ideal world, and by pretending otherwise, people get into trouble.

In recent years, we have seen hundreds of thousands of women and children slip from lives of relative comfort into lives of poverty and desperation. Like it or not, the time has come for every adult to take responsibility for his or her own financial survival. As too many Americans have already learned, the government, or a lifetime partner, cannot be depended upon to help. And we've already talked about the unfortunate shortage of good fairies and charming princes.

That is why this chapter is so important. It is not meant to glorify materialism, conspicuous consumption, or a simple lust for money. Rather, it attempts to bring the subject of money "out of the closet" so that students can examine their financial needs and their feelings about money. It demonstrates the role finances play in decision making and career choice, and suggests a variety of possible ways in which money can be used to make mixing career and family a less daunting task.

Melody's Budget

PAGE 43 **Workbook 20-22**

Objective:

To compare the impact of income on lifestyle and parenting choices.

Presentation Suggestions:

In preparation, check to see what AFDC payments and food stamp allotments are in your state and make the necessary revisions in the first budget provided. Then go over this example with the class, explaining each category and what might be included within it.

Collect and bring to class a box of resources for price information, including want ads, catalogs and bills which indicate utility costs, insurance rates, and so on. Allow students to use these materials to complete the three other budgets. Follow with class discussion of the questions on p. 46.

Follow-Up:

If your class needs more detailed information on budgeting, see Chapter Three of *Choices, Challenges*, or *Changes*, pp. 45 to 49 of this guide.

For more advanced classes, collect issues of *Money Magazine* and have students examine the monthly feature, "One Family's Finances."

Ask the male students in the class, "If you found yourself in Melody's predicament, an unskilled single parent, what would you do and what kind of job could you get?" They are likely to say they wouldn't be unskilled, and that they would find a higher-paying, blue-collar job.

Debate/discuss why poverty in the United States is a female/child issue.

Income Expectation Survey

PAGES 49-55 **Workbook 23-26**

Objective:

To help students clarify the relationship between their income expectations and their personal values, as well as the relationship between income expectations and career choice.

Presentation Suggestions:

Have students complete the exercise and compute their own scores. Be sure to emphasize beforehand that there are no right or wrong answers, but that the point of the survey is to help each student gain insight into his or her own feelings about money and expectations of what it can do. Remind them that their feelings can change with time and circumstances, so it might be a good idea to come back and retake this exercise from time to time.

Follow- Up:

Discuss each category and what it might mean in terms of career choice.

Activities:

Ask the class to guess in which category each of the fictional characters below might score highest:

Alex Keaton on “Family Ties”

Jessica Fletcher on "Murder She Wrote"

The Simpsons on “The Simpsons”

Al Bundy on “Married With Children”

The women on “Designing Women”

Murphy Brown on “Murphy Brown”

Arnie Becker on “LA Law”

Roxanne on “LA Law”

Coach Fox on "Coach"

Income Expectations and Career Choice

PAGE 56 Workbook 27

Objective:

To help students begin to see the importance of considering income expectations along with career choices.

Presentation Suggestions:

Ask students to think of careers that would be consistent with the various income expectation categories. Then have them list careers that would probably not be good choices for each category. Some possibilities:

Helping Others:

Good choices: Physical therapist, fire fighter, psychiatrist, financial planner, brain surgeon, medical researcher, comedian, nutritionist, speech pathologist, police officer, sales clerk.

Bad choices: Weapons researcher, loan shark, bill collector, auto repossessor.

Measure of Success:

Good choices: Politician, stockbroker, writer, fund-raiser, manager, weather forecaster, professional athlete, lawyer, sales representative, real estate agent.

Bad choices: Social worker, file clerk, phone installer, house painter, chimney sweep.

Power and Prestige:

Good choices: President of the United States, Supreme Court justice, U.S. senator, chief executive officer of a major corporation, newspaper editor, heart surgeon, bank president.

Bad choices: Garbage collector, delivery person, bank teller, street sweeper, factory worker, store clerk, used car salesperson.

Purchasing Power:

Good choices: Entrepreneur, CPA, plastic surgeon, dentist, business executive.

Bad choices: Waitress, secretary, receptionist, nurse, cosmetologist, cafeteria worker.

Security:

Good choices: Mortician, obstetrician, government worker, garbage collector, tax preparer.

Bad choices: Stock-broker, entrepreneur, rock star, poet, politician.

Freedom:

Good choices: Artist, carpenter, explorer, nature photographer, anthropologist.

Bad choices: Accountant, emergency room doctor, member of the military, presidential adviser.

Unfortunate Necessity:

Good choices: Anything you want to do that pays enough to support you.

Bad choices: Anything you don't want to do, or that doesn't pay a livable wage.

Personal Values Survey
Assessing Your Career Values

PAGE 57 **Workbook 28**

Objective:

To help students realize that there are many important considerations in making a career choice, and that their personal values need to mesh with their income expectations if they are to find their work rewarding.

Presentation Suggestions:

Have students respond personally to each of the questions.

Follow-Up:

For more in-depth work on values clarification in relation to career choice, see the pp. 88-105 in Chapter Four of *Choices, Challenges,* or *Changes.*

Money and Decision Making
How Does Money Affect Your Decisions?

PAGES 58-60   Workbook 29-30

Objective:

To create a greater awareness of the ways in which students' feelings about money will affect the decisions they make in almost any area of their lives.

Presentation Suggestions:

Have students work through the exercise, picking the response they think would most clearly match their own reasoning in each situation. Then ask them to total the number of "a" responses, "b" responses, and so on. Each letter corresponds to one of the income expectation categories from the earlier exercise.

Some students will have chosen the same letter response in most situations. They show a consistency of thought that will make it easier to decide on a course of action when both finances and personal values are involved. It will be easier to choose an appropriate career that will meet their income expectations.

Other students may have picked a variety of letter responses, with no clear preference for any category. These students are more likely to have problems meshing career decisions with income expectations. Careful evaluation will be necessary.

Activities:

Survey the class. What percentage of the class scored highest in each of the seven categories? Now break that down by gender and compare the results. Were there any major differences between the males and the females of the class? In which category did the majority of the males score highest? In which did the majority of the women score highest? Why do you think this happened?

Chapter Four

Like money, time and flexibility are generally in short supply among working parents. This chapter attempts to show how career choice impacts on options for parenting. Those careers offering more free time and higher flexibility (and more money, too) allow parents to operate effectively in both their work and family-oriented tasks.

At this point in the course, students should begin to see that their work lives and family lives are inevitably intertwined, and that careful planning of both is a necessary element for a satisfying life. This chapter is key in motivating students (especially young women) to pursue a career in which they could support a family and still have time enough to be a parent.

Time – Your Finite Resource

PAGES 65-73 **Workbook 31**

Objective:

To make time seem more real and finite than we often think it is, and to start students thinking about how much they can realistically hope to accomplish in a 24-hour period.

Presentation Suggestions:

Olympia's day is charted in the book to serve as an example of a typical day for a woman working part-time. Ask students to examine this diagram and note how much time Olympia devotes to her various tasks (and what they are). Then have them fill in the empty circle to show how a woman working full-time might allot the hours at her disposal. If she allows eight hours for sleep and eight hours for work (plus time to get dressed, commuting time and lunch time), does she have many choices about the way she spends the remaining part of her day?

Follow-Up:

Ask students to share their charts during group discussion. What parts of Barbara's life are most apt to be shortchanged? Did anyone come up with creative ways for Barbara to spend her time?

Activities:

Poll the young men in the class. Would they have completed this chart differently if asked to complete it for themselves, and if they were working full-time with a child? Have the students draw a time line illustrating a typical day in a single father's life. Where are the differences in time arrangement most obvious for a single mother and a single father?

Time and the Single Parent

PAGE 67 **Workbook 32**

Objective:

To show how being the only adult in the house compounds the problems of the single parent, and to help students begin to relate to those problems. For students who are already experiencing this situation, the exercise may help them set new priorities and reorganize their day.

Presentation Suggestions:

Again, have students complete the chart and follow with group discussion.

Time Is Money

PAGES 68-73 **Workbook 32-35**

Objective:

To help students begin to see what salary can mean in actual time gained for parenting.

Presentation Suggestions:

Ask students to look closely at the list of average hourly salaries for some common careers. You might ask them to make separate lists — one of careers paying less than $10 per hour, one of careers paying more than that amount. What do the low-paying jobs have in common? What about those paying more? To illustrate the importance of education or training, compare the salaries of a store clerk and a physician — the doctor had to have a great deal of training, but she/he makes about ten times the salary of the clerk!

Then have the class fill in the daily salaries in the blanks provided. Note that for the higher-paying careers, students are asked to compute daily salary based on a *four*-hour day. Again, have the class compare the two lists of professions — this time based on the amount of *time* people in these fields must work in order to make a living wage.

Use the graph to help illustrate how higher-paying jobs allow parents to have more time and flexibility in their lives. Then discuss the questions on pp. 70-71 in class. Students might now be aware of the relationship between time and money.

One more step: Often, young people think that having a job — any job — will allow them to support their families. If they cannot earn enough at one job, they most often consider taking on a second position. By completing the circle graph for a single parent with two jobs, the class should see that this is not a workable option, at least not one compatible with good parenting.

Being a Parent Is a Job

PAGES 72-75 **Workbook 36-38**

Objective:

To compare the relative flexibility of careers requiring more training with those requiring less training.

Presentation Suggestions:

Work through the exercise as a group, or have students do it on their own. Then discuss the questions that follow.

What pattern do you see emerging from the responses?

Higher-paying careers are usually more flexible.

Do careers with flexible schedules require more preparation and education?

Definitely.

Which type of career generally pays more?

A flexible career.

Can you explain the relationship between salary level and job flexibility? Can you think of reasons why this relationship exists?

Some possibilities:

- The more flexible jobs have most often been held by men, who design their careers to fit their own needs.
- Highly skilled workers are in a better position to negotiate for these kinds of benefits, because employers know the employee could easily quit and find another job.
- Unskilled workers have few alternatives, and so must do the jobs, or work the hours, others find undesirable.

Follow-Up:

Ask students to think of ways employers might make traditional, inflexible jobs more responsive to the needs of working parents. Job sharing? Flex time? Allowing employees to work at home?

Invite a panel of parents with careers of differing levels of flexibility to discuss how their work fits in with their family life — and how it doesn't.

In a co-ed class, split the class into male/female pairs. Pretend each pair is married with children. Let them decide the number. Ask them each to choose a career and then draw time circles for each partner. Have each pair report back to the class.

- How many young women chose to work part-time?
- How many young men chose to work part-time?
- How did they divide the child-care duties?
- Did the pairs exhibit traditional or nontraditional work/family patterns? (Were more young men wanting time with children, and therefore choosing part-time work?)

In class discussion, be sure to define the terms "traditional" and "nontraditional."

Chapter Five

In this chapter, students are introduced to some of the job categories that have the potential to work best for young parents in terms of salary, time and flexibility. Students can, at this point, begin to formulate a specific plan for achieving the kind of life they most desire.

While all these fields offer some attractive options, not every job *within* each field is compatible with parenting. This is an important point to emphasize. An emergency room doctor leads a much different life than a podiatrist; a real estate salesperson can spend more time at home than a manufacturer's representative; and owning and operating a huge conglomerate is more than a full-time job.

Professions

PAGES 80-81 **Workbook 39**

Objective:

To illustrate how high-paying careers are desirable for a person wishing to work part-time, because they pay well enough for a parent to support a family. Students should observe, however, that these are careers requiring extensive education and planning. By committing themselves now to prepare carefully for their futures, young people give themselves the most options for parenting in later life.

Presentation Suggestions:

Have students compute half-time salaries for the professions listed by dividing annual salaries by two. Then ask them to turn back to the budgets on pp. 43-46 and compare the budget they found most adequate in Chapter Three with those half-time salaries. If the half-time salaries are about equal to, or greater than, the budgeted figure in Chapter Three, have students circle the "yes" in column 4.

Follow with a group discussion. Some good questions to ask:

What do these careers have in common besides high salary?

They require a lot of education.

It is often difficult to be admitted to these professional programs.

They require high school and college math.

If these careers mix so well with raising, a family, why are there so few women in the professions?

Until the late 1970s, sex discrimination kept many women out of professional programs in college and beyond.

Women still often do not believe they will have to earn a living, and so do not consider careers requiring a great deal of educational commitment.

Young women who do not take advanced math in high school or junior college automatically eliminate themselves from consideration by professional schools.

Free-Lancer

PAGES 83-85 **Workbook 40**

Objective:

To get students thinking beyond the obvious about career choices and to show the range of flexibility possible if people approach their work in a creative manner.

Presentation Suggestions:

Ask students to think of possible free-lance careers for people working in the fields listed. This can be done by students on their own or as a class exercise. How many ideas can they come up with?

Some possibilities:

Sales clerk: Running a shopping service, being a wardrobe consultant, being an independent sales representative (for a company like Mary Kay Cosmetics, for example).

Graphic artist: Starting an advertising agency, designing books, greeting cards, business cards or stationery.

Police officer: Starting a security service, becoming a private detective, teaching self-defense.

Airline pilot: Giving flying lessons, flying corporate jets, starting a charter flight service.

Professional athlete: Becoming a personal trainer, giving lessons in his or her sport, presenting seminars on physical fitness and wellness.

Groundskeeper: Starting a lawn service, consulting with builders or landscape architects, giving lectures on lawn care and gardening, writing a gardening column for a local newspaper.

Hotel maid: Working as a private housekeeper, starting a cleaning service, setting up an agency to place housekeepers.

Follow-Up:

Invite a successful free-lancer with a family to tell the class about his or her experiences and answer questions. This person should be someone to whom the class can relate, someone from a background similar to theirs who has become successful. This person could serve as a role model for the class.

Sales

PAGES 86-87 **Workbook 41**

Objective:

To have students stretch their imaginations again by thinking of as many possibilities for work in the field of sales as they can.

Presentation Suggestions:

Brainstorm this exercise in class. Make a list on the board of as many kinds of sales as the class can come up with. Encourage students to think beyond the traditional types of sales (clerking in a store, for example) that usually offer low pay. There are many opportunities for women in sales positions that pay quite well, even for women without a great deal of education. It's important that the class sees this as a field of much potential.

When you've completed your list, you might ask students to divide it into sales positions likely to offer higher pay or lower pay; then into sales positions likely to be compatible or incompatible with parenting. (Positions requiring a lot of travel are usually not good for parents with young children.)

Follow-Up:

Again, invite a guest speaker. Make it someone who has done well in a nontraditional sales position.

Consulting

PAGES 88-89 **Workbook 41**

Objective:

To have students examine the field to see if it holds any possibilities for their future.

Presentation Suggestions:

How much time you devote to this section will depend upon your class. If you have a highly motivated group, they may find this field intriguing. For less motivated students, it does not hold much potential.

Ask students to consider their own skills and personalities before answering the list of questions "yes" or "no." This will also encourage them to begin thinking about their personal characteristics, which, of course, must be considered in relation to any career choice.

Follow-Up:

If consulting seems a distinct possibility for your class, you may want to have a guest speaker or panel of consultants who can answer questions about this career field.

Manager

PAGES 90-92 **Workbook 42**

Objective:

Once again, to evaluate personal skills and characteristics, and what they might mean for a career in management.

Presentation Suggestions:

Have students consider the list of statements and decide whether, at this point in their lives, each phrase is "very true," "sometimes true," or "not true."

Follow-Up:

In Chapter Seven, students will learn some skills that may help them change their answers from "not true" to "very true," if they are motivated to do so. At that point, have them turn back to this exercise and think of ways they could apply the "5 Cs" to become better candidates for management positions.

You may, once more, want to invite people with various kinds of jobs in management to come in, individually or as a panel, to talk about how this career field works for parents. Chances are, they will report that there is not a great deal of flexibility, but that their income allows them to hire help for some of their family responsibilities and to afford quality child care.

Resources:

Farley, Jennie, ed. *The Woman in Management: Career and Family Issues.* Cornell University, New York: ILR Press, 1983.

Sadker, D. and Sadker, M. Sexism in American education: The hidden curriculum. In L.R. Wolfe (Ed.), *Women, Work and School: Occupational Segregation and the Role of Education.* Boulder, CO; Westview, 1991.

Entrepreneurial Checklist

PAGES 96-97 **Workbook 43-44**

Objective:

To have students evaluate the attitudes and skills necessary to become an entrepreneur.

Presentation Suggestion:

The very word "entrepreneur" may make this field sound unattainable to all but the most motivated and exceptional students, but this is not the case. In class discussion after students mark the checklist, be sure to emphasize that opportunities exist at all levels of skill and education and that, in many communities, a woman can, for example, make more money as a housekeeper than she could as a clerk in a local boutique. Forty percent of all entrepreneurs have only a high school degree or less. Of course, there are no limits on how far someone can go with an enterprise. Thousands of women are starting their own businesses every year, in part because financial rewards can be greater than if they are working for someone else, and in part because of the degree of flexibility available to entrepreneurs once their business is established. Of course, men, too, can find career satisfaction and more options for parenting as entrepreneurs.

Follow-Up:

Another opportunity for guest speakers. Try to find someone whose achievements will seem realistic to your class.

Activities:

As a homework assignment ask students to decide on a business they would like to start sometime in their lives; then have them write a paper about that business and why they feel it would be successful.

Also see the Corporate Game on p. 101 of this *Instructor's Guide*.

Resources:

Comiskey, James C. *How to Start, Expand and Sell a Business: A Complete Guidebook for Entrepreneurs*. San Jose, California: Venture Perspective Press, 1986. (4300 Stevens Creek Blvd., Suite 155-A, San Jose, CA 95129)

The Technological Age

PAGES 100-101 **Workbook 45**

Objective:

To get students thinking creatively about the uses of technology and whether they have an affinity for working with it. Also, to help them realize that they will have to deal with technology, like it or not.

Presentation Suggestions:

Divide students into small groups and assign each group to consider two or three of the careers listed. Bring the group back together for discussion.

What technical backgrounds or abilities are needed in these fields today?

Manager: Keyboarding, data processing, programming

Homemaker: Using a microwave, programming appliances

Court reporter: Keyboarding

Nurse: Keyboarding, operating computerized equipment

Schoolteacher: Keyboarding, programming

Shop clerk: Using a price scanner

Receptionist: Using an electronic switchboard

Newspaper reporter: Keyboarding, word processing

Graphic artist: Keyboarding, using computerized graphics

Architect: Keyboarding, using computerized graphics

Pharmacist: Keyboarding, data searching

Police officer: Keyboarding

How has technology made these jobs easier or more enjoyable?

Less need for paperwork

Easier access to needed information

More time for pleasurable parts of the job

How might computers have changed these jobs by the year 2000?

Brainstorm this part of the exercise as a class, if necessary. Encourage students to let their imaginations run wild.

Manager: TV phone systems,"teleconferencing" — no need to travel to meetings

Homemaker: robotic servant, "programmable" households

Court reporter: recorded on video micro chip, with automatic written text production on request

Nurse: personalized robot to dispense medication for each patient

Schoolteacher: interactive video and computer

Store clerk: automatic checkout, scanning and bagging

Receptionist: robot replaces receptionist

Newspaper reporter: voice-activated word processor

Graphic artist: computerized graphics, using wand on screen

Pharmacist: calibrated wand to determine correct dosage and medication for each individual

Police officer: heat-sensitive laser scanner to find hidden suspects

Resources:

Goldberg, Joan R. *High-Tech Career Strategies for Women.* New York: Macmillan, 1984.

If You're Not Going to College

PAGES 102-103 **No Workbook Page**

Objective:

To help students realize there are many career opportunities compatible with making an adequate salary and raising a family that do not require a college degree. The class should observe, however, that the element of planning is still important.

Presentation Suggestions:

Discuss the pros and cons of vocations listed on p. 103.

Follow-up:

Ask a vocational adviser to speak to the class about opportunities in these careers, consider the education required, salary and flexibility.

Have someone who followed this career route address the class.

Invite a military recruiter to speak to the class. Ask him/her to address the issue of mixing a military career and family and to comment on Gloria's Story, p. 102.

How much time you give this issue depends upon the population with which you are working. If most of your students are not going to college, invite a number of speakers who have careers that do not require a college degree and who mix career and family successfully.

Instructor's Notes:

Chapter Six

We often don't realize the impact outside forces have on the personal choices we make. The purpose of this chapter is to help students realize that their friends, their families, and society in general may have skewed their thoughts concerning what is possible or necessary for them to do. Girls, especially, are prone to make self-limiting choices. We hope that if they are aware of the powerful forces at work outside themselves, they will be better able to draw from their inner strength and knowledge to make wise decisions for their future.

The Wage Gap Quiz

PAGES 107-110 **Workbook 46**

Objective:

To once again use "startling statements" to look at the wage gap and help students become more aware of its existence. Turn to p. 164 in this guide to review the procedure.

Presentation Suggestions:

Have students answer the questions to the best of their ability; discuss the answers in class.

Activities:

Choose students from the class to debate what can be done about the wage gap. One team will take the position that, "Women need to change their career strategies if they hope to earn an equal wage." The other team will defend the statement, "Society needs to change in order for women to earn an equal wage." Have the teams research their positions and present their arguments to the class. Follow with a group discussion.

Childhood Choices

PAGES 111-113 **Workbook 47**

Objective:

To help the class realize how society has conditioned them to act in certain ways, and to evaluate how this conditioning may be affecting present and future choices.

Presentation Suggestions:

Ask students to answer the questions based on their personal experiences. Follow with group discussion and have class members reflect on their own upbringing and evaluate how it has affected their thinking about appropriate behavior or career choice.

Poll the students. Did more males give predominantly "b" answers?

Ask the young women who had a majority of "b" answers to reflect and evaluate what encourages these tendencies in their lives.

Follow-Up:

Assign students to write a short essay about a personal choice made in the past year (what classes to take, what activities to participate in, and the like), explaining what factors were considered before making their choice. Have them conclude by stating whether or not they would make the same choice if they had it to do over again.

Resources:

Nicholson, Heather Johnston. *Facts and Reflections on Careers for Today's Girls,* 1985. Girls Inc. National Resource Center, 411 West Michigan Street, Indianapolis, IN 46202.

Girls Incorporated, *Past the Pink and Blue Predicament: Freeing the Next Generation from Sex Stereotypes.* 441 West Michigan St., Indianapolis, IN, 46202: Author, 1992

American Association of University Women Educational Foundation, *How Schools Shortchange Girls,* 1411 16th St. N.W., Washington, D.C. 20036-4873

Sadker, Myra and David, *Failing at Fairness, How America's Schools Cheat Girls,* Charles Scribners & Sons, Macmillan Publishing Company, 866 Third Avenue, New York, NY 10022, 1994

Conduct a Personal Survey

PAGES 114-115 **Workbook 48-49**

Objective:

To personalize and evaluate how personal environment may affect thoughts or choices.

Presentation Suggestions:

Have each student list the names of two women friends, classmates, or family members, along with the career title each holds or is preparing for. Then have the student evaluate whether each career is traditionally held by more men, more women, or about equal numbers of each. Using this information to complete the "news release" provided will help the class personalize and analyze its findings.

Activity:

Combine the individual surveys to form a larger sample, which might provide more statistically accurate numbers. Have the class write a news release reflecting its findings, and offer it to the school paper or local newspaper for publication as a class study.

Vocational Education, the Best-Kept Secret

PAGES 118-119 **Workbook 50-51**

Objective:

To illustrate that most traditionally male, blue-collar careers pay more than traditionally female careers that require college degrees.

Presentation Suggestions:

Ask students to indicate in the columns provided whether the listed careers require a college or vocational education. Then have them compare the average annual salaries of the careers they've placed in each column and enter these on the graph that follows. Students should be able to see easily that, even though the "women's" jobs require a college education, they pay less than "men's" work not requiring college training.

Activity:

Have another debate. This time the positions are, "Things are fair as they stand: People performing these blue-collar jobs should be paid more than the college-educated workers listed," and "It's not fair: Careers requiring more education should pay more, whether they are performed by a man or a woman." Follow with group discussion.

Resources:

Kosterlitz, Julie, and Florence Graves. "Should Nurses Be Paid as Much as Truck Drivers?": Debate between Betty Friedan and Phyllis Schlafly. *Common Cause,* March/April 1983, pp. 36-39.

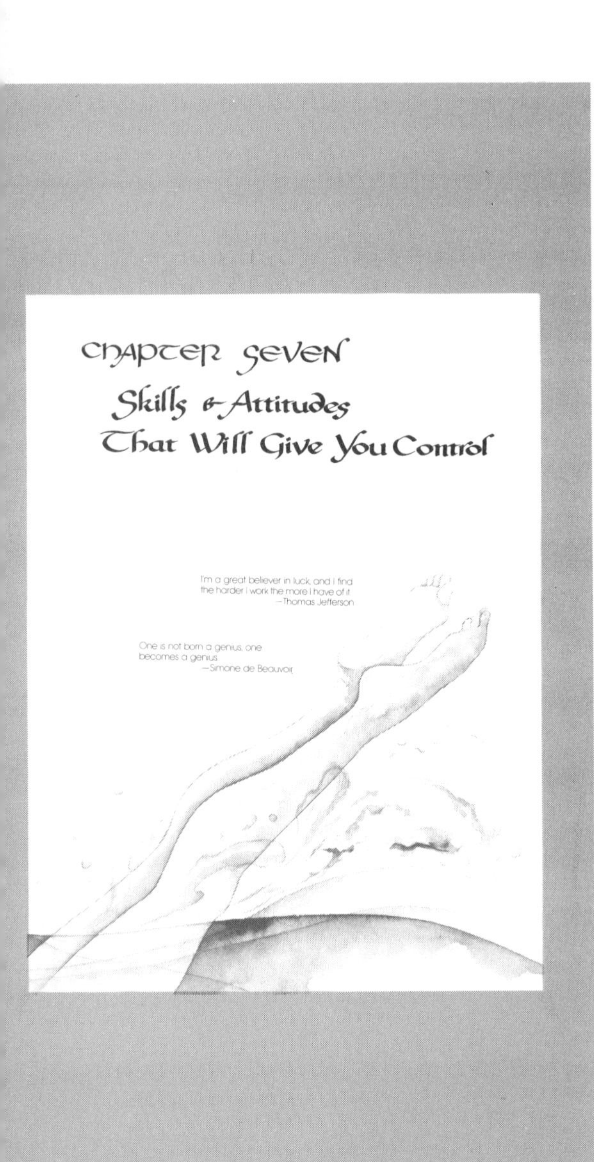

Chapter Seven

In the first half of this book, students dealt to a large extent with facts, figures and ideas. In Chapter Seven, they concentrate more on themselves and their personal plans. They examine the skills and personality traits that most successful and content people have in common, think about which of these skills and characteristics they already have, and start to develop a plan for gaining those they see lacking in their own lives.

In short, this chapter will help students feel that they have control over their lives. Without this belief, few people of any age will venture forth, take calculated risks, or pursue their dreams. And, of course, without self-confidence and effort, dreams do not come true.

Competence

PAGES 128-129 **Workbook 52**

Objective:

To help students identify their skills and plan to work toward greater competency.

Presentation Suggestions:

This section deals principally with skills identification and goal setting. If the class needs more detailed instructions, see Chapters Four and Eight in *Choices* and *Challenges,* and p. 58 and p. 89 of this *Instructor's Guide*.

Commitment

PAGES 130-131 **Workbook 53**

Objective:

To help students have a greater understanding of commitment and begin to think about what is most important in *their* lives.

Presentation Suggestions:

This section requires a great deal of discussion. Be sure to equate commitment with persistence. It is easy to keep a commitment when nothing prevents it, but the true importance of the term becomes apparent when obstacles are placed in the way. It is those who persist, those whose commitment is strong enough, who eventually overcome those problems and reach their goals. Emphasize that few things worth having in life come easily and that commitment in itself can be an extremely rewarding part of anyone's life.

Follow-Up:

Invite a guest speaker who has made a commitment to something, someone who encountered obstacles, refused to give up and eventually succeeded. Someone who has overcome an obvious handicap would be ideal.

Confidence

PAGES 132-133 **Workbook 54**

Objective:

To teach affirmations as a tool in acquiring or keeping self-confidence.

Presentation Suggestions:

Ask students to think of situations in which they need to gain confidence and write affirmations that might help them do so.

Follow-Up:

In group discussion, have the students share their affirmations so that others who may need to work on similar problems can learn from their classmates.

Activities:

Pass out 3 x 5 cards and have students write their affirmations, one on each card. Instruct them to take the cards home and tape them on their mirrors so that, every time they brush their teeth or comb their hair, they can repeat these positive statements. Every week or so for the remainder of the course, inquire whether they are still doing their affirmations and ask whether anyone has noticed any difference in their own feelings or behavior. Try to create a supportive environment, so that those who are having problems of some kind can come to the class and be assured of getting encouragement and positive reinforcement.

Creativity

PAGES 134-136 **Workbook 55**

Objective:

To teach students the steps of creativity and to help them realize that creativity is not the province of a special few, but simply a way of approaching a problem with an open mind.

Presentation Suggestions:

Ask students to use the steps described to come up with innovative solutions to a personal problem.

Activities:

To get creative juices flowing, bring a common item to class and let the students brainstorm possible uses for it. The item might be a coat hanger, a match box, a roll of paper towels, a bar of soap, or anything else that comes to mind. List all the class suggestions on the board, then let the group decide which is best.

Or divide the class into smaller groups and let each group come up with its own list and its own candidate for best use. Bring the class back together to share ideas and vote on the most creative idea. Perhaps offer a prize to the individual or group with the greatest number of ideas or the best ideas.

Resources:

De Bono, Edward, and Michael de Saint-Arnaud. *The Learn-To-Think Coursebook.* 2d ed. New York: Edward de Bono School of Thinking, 1982.

Hunt, Morgan. "Seven Steps to Better Thinking," *Reader's Digest,* April 1983.

Courage

PAGES 137-139 **Workbook 56-57**

Objective:

To have students evaluate their own risk-taking skills and learn how to take calculated risks.

Presentation Suggestions:

Have students work through the exercise in the book to plan whether and how to do something they think they want to do, but have not had the courage to pursue.

Follow-Up:

In class discussion, ask students to share courageous decisions they have been called on to make in their lives.

Or have as a guest speaker someone who has made a courageous decision and seen it through, especially someone who made a courageous career decision.

If the class needs more information on risk taking or assertiveness, see Chapters Five and Six in *Choices, Challenges* and *Changes*.

Resources:

Viscott, David, M.D. *Risking*. New York: Pocket Books, 1979.

The Importance of Math

PAGE 140 **No Workbook Page**

The math exercises in *More Choices* are designed to meet three goals. First, they should make students aware of the amount — or lack — of support they have had from their families, teachers and friends in regard to their performance in math classes. Young people are notorious for wanting to be "like everyone else." Since there is often peer pressure to avoid math and little support from parents and teachers to do well in it (for young women, at least), students often sabotage their own futures by avoiding or failing in math.

Second, the exercises ask students to examine their own attitudes about math and their ability to do well in it. Negative thoughts often make for self-fulfilling prophecies.

Third, students need to understand the importance of math in terms of future career choices, earning potential and job flexibility.

As you go through this section of the book, emphasize these points and, as the old song has it, "accentuate the positive." Even if students have not done well in math in the past, there are steps they can take to gain important math skills.

Attitude = Success

PAGE 141 **Workbook 58**

Objective:

To have students examine the amount of encouragement to do well in math they have received throughout their educational career.

Presentation Suggestions:

Ask students to think back to their earliest years in math class. How did the teacher present the subject? Was it difficult? Easy? Fun? What kind of grades did they earn? What grades did their friends earn? Did they have homework? Did their parents help them with their homework? Did their parents take an interest in their grades?

Have class members try to recall as much as they can, and then try to trace how all these elements changed (if they did) through each succeeding year of school. Then ask them to mark their own attitudes and expectations, and those of their parents and teachers, for each year on the chart provided. They should use a different kind of pen or colored ink for each category (self, parents and teachers).

The result should be a kind of flow chart. For many women, especially, the flow will be decidedly downward. They may have started out with good feelings about math, but as they grew older, their attitudes and expectations took on a negative cast. And their grades probably fell along with their hopes to excel. For young men the inverse is often true.

Have the class note, too, whether or not their teachers and parents shared the same attitudes and expectations. Can students draw any conclusions from this? Do they see any relationship between their grades and attitudes? If there is a relationship, students should be encouraged to believe that, by improving their attitude, they can improve their math competence as well.

Have the class assess how those proficient in math are presented in the media and popular culture. Often "math whizzes" and scientists are presented as socially inept and "nerds". Of course, women in the sciences are perceived as masculine or unable to "get dates."

Activities:

Have the class brainstorm ways of getting more support for doing well in math. Perhaps they could form a support group, get a tutor, or take special remedial classes or a class dealing with math anxiety.

For more activities, see *Choices, Challenges* and *Changes* curriculum, Chapter Nine and see p. 95 in this *Instructor's Guide*.

Getting in Shape for Math Success

PAGE 142 Workbook 59

Objective:

To allow the student to practice positive affirmations in a real-life setting, and develop a better attitude toward math.

Presentation Suggestions:

Have students read the affirmations provided, and then write some of their own, using the skill they gained earlier in the chapter. Ask them to choose their three favorite math affirmations, put them on 3 x 5 cards, and tape them to their mirrors along with their other affirmations as a daily reminder to keep repeating them.

Activities:

Sponsor a math poster contest that incorporates an affirmation about math with colorful graphics.

Follow-Up:

After a few weeks, ask if anyone in class has improved at math or made a change in plans regarding math. Throughout the course, remind students occasionally to keep repeating their affirmations. Share this exercise with the math instructors in your institution and encourage their support.

Math – The Critical Filter

PAGE 143 Workbook 60

Objective:

To point out why math is important to students' future careers.

Presentation Suggestions:

Have students note the listed careers that require a math background, and ask them to return to p. 75 to compare the average annual salaries of those careers requiring math with those not requiring math.

Follow with group discussion. Students should see that there is a strong connection between the math requirement and income expectations. This is not surprising. After all, they have been told throughout the course that, if they expect to make an adequate salary, they will need to *prepare* for a job, not just *get* one. Planning and education — whether at the college or vocational level — are the most important indicators of future earnings.

Then, have the class turn to the chart on p. 75 and compare the relative flexibility of the careers requiring and not requiring math.

This relationship may be less evident. But, given some thought, it makes sense, too. We have already seen that jobs traditionally held by men tend to pay more and tend to be more flexible. Now we see that they often requiring a math background as well. Since women are less likely to have a solid math education, they are often unqualified to hold these jobs. They are likely to earn less money at less flexible careers. It becomes easy to see the importance of math for anyone hoping to mix career and family life.

A Word Problem

PAGES 144-146 **Workbook 61-63**

Objective:

To show the future value of a math education in a very concrete manner by putting a dollar value on every hour spent studying math, and to show how math plays a part in disparate parts of our lives, including decision making.

Presentation Suggestions:

Work through the problem with the class. An example is provided below.

If math required an average of 5 (a) hours of studying math per week, how many hours of study would be required to complete four years of math? Each school year is 36 weeks.

4 years x 36 weeks x 5 (a) hours studying math per week = 720 (b) total hours spent studying math in high school.

According to the United States Department of Labor, the average teenage woman can expect to spend 27 years in the workforce. How many years do you think you will spend in the workforce between the ages of 18 and 65?

30 (c) years

If a full-time job takes 2,080 hours per year (40 hours per week x 52 weeks per year), how many hours could you work in your career over a lifetime?

30 (c) years in the workforce x 2,080 work hours per year = 62,400 (d) hours worked in your lifetime.

What is the ratio between the hours spent studying math in high school and the total number of hours spent in your career?

62,400 (d) divided by 720 (b) = 86.66 (e)

Therefore, for every hour you spend studying math in high school, you will spend how many hours in the workforce?

86.66 (e)

Choose a career from the list on p. 143 that does not require math and that you have some interest in. Then turn to p. 74 and calculate the average hourly rate of pay and enter below.

Career title: Shop clerk = $4.50 (s) average hourly rate of pay.

Now choose a career requiring either high school or college math from the same list on p. 143. It, too, should hold some appeal for you. Again, turn to p. 74 and calculate the average hourly salary.

Career title: Elementary school teacher = $9.86 (r) average hourly rate of pay.

To determine how much each hour of studying in high school is worth in dollars of future earnings, first determine the difference in hourly wages between the two careers above.

$9.86 (r) - $4.50 (s) = $5.36 (t)

Next, multiply that difference by the total number of hours you can expect to hold a job — figure (d) from the previous page. This will give you the difference in lifetime earnings between the job that requires a strong math background and the one that does not.

62,400 (d) x $5.36 (t) = $334,464.00 (w)

One more way to look at this is to divide; the difference in lifetime earnings (w) by the number of hours spent studying math (b) in order to get the increased future earnings for every hour spent studying math in high school.

$334,464.00 (w) divided by 720 (b) = $464.53 of increased future earnings for every hour spent studying math in high school.

Calculators would be helpful for this problem if they are available. Ask each student to share his/her last two figures, difference in lifetime earnings and earnings for every hour spent studying math. Be sure to emphasize the last point. As your students leave the classroom, remind them how much they may get in future earnings for their math homework that evening.

If you are working with a college age or re-entry population, spend another class hour presenting strategies for getting the math background needed for better careers.

Putting Your Skills to Use and Your Own Planning Model

PAGES 148-151 Workbook 64-67

Objective:

To give students further practice in using the 5 Cs of control. This could also be used as a test.

Presentation Suggestions:

The first exercise is meant to help students use the 5 Cs to improve their math ability. Ask them to think about their own strengths and weaknesses as far as math is concerned, and then complete the exercise. Follow up with class discussion. Some examples of possible steps include:

Competence:

Evaluate my math aptitude and attitude.

Discuss my need for math with school counselor.

Register for advanced math classes for the remainder of my high school career.

Ask for special help if I need it.

Commitment:

A commitment to do well in math usually requires persistence. Someone who has had trouble with the subject in the past may need to go back and retake some courses, take remedial courses, or get a tutor. A student committed to do well in math will ask the teacher to explain a concept that he or she does not grasp, rather than pretend to understand. A committed math student will do the assignments, even if it means giving up some other activity he or she finds more desirable. This student will not give up, even if the first few months in class are difficult and frustrating. He or she will continue to ask questions, get special help and continue to work by him/herself.

Confidence:

I, Judy, am capable of doing well at in math.

I, John, always do my math homework.

I, Judy, am willing to work hard, ask questions and get special help.

I, John, see math as an important part of a sound education.

I, Judy, can go far as I like with my math education.

Creativity:

Ways to achieve math goals:

Ask friends who do well at math to help; form a support group with friends who share my commitment to math; get a tutor; ask the teacher for assistance; ask my parents for help; get a part-time job requiring math competence; read math books on my own; strike up a friendship with someone who thinks math is fascinating; take a remedial math course; take an evening class in math; go to a seminar on math anxiety; keep my checkbook balanced; stop using a calculator.

Possible problems:

I don't like math; I don't understand math; I don't have time to learn math.

Possible solutions:

Use affirmations to convince myself I like and understand math; clear my schedule to make time for math; ask for help from a teacher or someone who does well at math; study the lives of successful people to see how math mattered to them; interview someone I admire and ask what role math has played in his/her life; commit one to two hours each night to math homework.

Courage:

What risks must you take? Are the risks worth the possible rewards? What is the worst thing that could happen to you if you try to improve your math background, but don't succeed?

The biggest risk is the risk of failure. Possible rewards, though, include increased self-esteem, increased options for mixing career and family, increased earning potential. The worst that can happen is that I will not become good at math and then . . . what? Will my friends or family disown me? Probably not. Will I catch some rare disease transmitted through fractions and decimal points? Probably not. Will I be any worse off than if I hadn't tried to succeed at math? Definitely not.

What is the best thing that could happen if you try?

I could learn to like math and excel at it, and go on to be admitted to the career program of my choice that requires a solid math background. I could then earn enough money to mix career and family and have enough time to enjoy them both.

Ask students to think of another goal or problem in their lives and use the planning model provided to come up with a plan to solve it.

Follow-Up:

Divide students into small groups and ask them to share their answers for the exercises. This will help them reaffirm some of the planning processes.

For the second exercise, ask two or three students to share their plan and explain the decision-making process they used to come to the conclusions they did.

Chapter Eight

Busy people — and all people attempting to mix career and family are busy — tend to lose the sense of balance so necessary to a satisfying life. Statistics show that women who work outside the home still tend to be largely responsible for child care and housework. This intensifies the demands upon their time and makes it probable that some other areas of their lives are getting short shrift. Men, on the other hand, have been more likely to devote excessive amounts of time to their work and to neglect their personal needs — a situation that has led to an epidemic of stress related conditions, none of them conducive to a rewarding lifestyle.

Chapter Eight introduces students a sense of balance. There is a need to pay careful attention to the needs of their families, the requirements of their careers, and the personal needs that are too often neglected. Most people do not seem to have an intrinsic ability to balance their lives — they must make a conscious effort to do so, stopping to evaluate how they are spending their time on a regular basis. This chapter provides some guidelines they might use to make their decisions and judge their progress.

Balancing Your Life

PAGES 156-159 **Workbook 68-69**

Objective:

To illustrate the importance of a balanced life and the many ways in which lives can become unbalanced.

Presentation Suggestions:

Discuss the definitions for the three spheres of life. What activities might fall into each category?

Examples:

Career — paid employment, volunteer work, raising children, keeping house, going to school, managing finances, making a transition from one location to another or one role to another, reading professional materials, attending seminars to network with others, getting career counseling, applying for a new job.

Relationships — dealing with spouse, children, or other family members, seeing friends, making phone calls or writing letters, buying gifts, preparing a special meal, providing a shoulder to cry on or an attentive ear to listen to problems.

Self — eating, sleeping, exercising, maintaining health, reading for pleasure, listening to music, taking vacations, meditating, watching TV, shopping, going to concerts, movies or the theater, getting a haircut, going to church or synagogue.

Have students complete the circle graphs for Joyce, Sally, or Patti, either individually or in small groups. Then ask them to write the story of someone whose life they think is well balanced, and to complete the chart of a woman they know whose life is out of balance. Finally, have them graph their own life. Follow with group discussion.

Follow-Up:

Poll the class to see which area in the lives of the women whose lives are out of balance is receiving too much attention and which area is neglected

Getting Control

PAGE 160 **No Workbook Page**

Objective:

To help students understand and deal with the concept of stress.

Presentation Suggestions:

Have students read through the section and follow with group discussion. If needed, refer to the assertiveness exercises in Chapter Six of *Choices, Challenges,* or *Changes* to help them learn to take control of their own lives; p. 72 of the *Instructor's Guide*.

Self-Health

PAGES 161-162 **Workbook 70**

Objective:

To give students an evaluation tool that helps them recognize how well they are treating themselves and what changes they may need to make.

Presentation Suggestions:

Young people may tend to scoff at these health considerations, but at least we are planting the seeds of awareness. Ask students to mark the column that most closely represents their own situation.

Follow-Up:

Have students give the same quiz to their parents. Follow with class discussion. What similarities arise? What are the potential long-term consequences of such behavior?

Ask a health professional to speak to the class, or bring in a variety of books and magazines on the topic of health and stress management.

Managing Your Time and Energy

PAGES 164-168 **Workbook 71-74**

Objective:

To illustrate the need for planning and setting priorities in keeping a life in balance. Also to provide a tool to help students accomplish this goal.

Presentation Suggestions:

Ask students to complete the first part of this exercise, then discuss. Points to bring out in class:

No one can do everything.

Each person needs to decide for her/himself what is most important.

The more time you spend on unimportant things, the less time you will have for the activities you most want or need to pursue.

To keep a life in balance, a person should schedule time for some activities from each of the three spheres.

Many tasks can be delegated to other family members or outside help.

The second half of the exercise allows students to personalize the priority-setting process by making their own list of activities and concerns. It also helps them see where they may be spending time unwisely and how well balanced their own lives are. Ask them to complete the exercises and follow with group discussion.

How many students think their lives are well balanced?

In lives which are out of balance, which sphere is most often given too much preference?

Too little?

Are students making time for the activities they think are most important?

If not, what are they doing instead?

Follow-Up:

Ask students to make a list of the three most important things for them to do — one from each sphere of activity — each day for a week or two. Then have them report back. Did they do the things they meant to get done? If so, how did this improve their lives? If not, why not?

Resources:

Schaevitz, Marjorie Hansen. *The Superwoman Syndrome*. New York: Warner Books, Inc., 1984.

So You Want to Be a Wonderwoman

PAGES 169-170 **Workbook 75**

Objective:

To help students evaluate their own potential for leading the life of what we have termed a "Wonderwoman."

Presentation Suggestions:

It is essential to define a Wonderwoman, and to explain how she differs from a Superwoman. As we see it, Superwoman is a myth created by the media, society, or whatever. Women see her held up as the ideal, assume that her lifestyle is not only possible but mandatory, and fall into the kinds of traps we discussed in Chapter One. A Wonderwoman, on the other hand, has certain physical and emotional characteristics that have led her to make a *conscious* choice to lead a very high-energy, high-achieving life.

Ask students to answer the eight questions as truthfully as possible. Stress that very few people of either sex can honestly answer "yes" to all of them, and that, even if they can, it is not necessary to follow this difficult path. It is simply a choice open to a few people, some of whom find it a rewarding way to live.

Follow-Up:

Do students know anyone they consider a Wonderwoman? If so, ask class members to have these people answer the same questionnaire.

Activities:

Invite one or more Wonderwomen to tell the class how they manage their time and why they chose the way of life they did. They are not easy to find. They are rare indeed.

Instructor's Notes:

Chapter Nine

Even though they live in the midst of a society now made up of working couples, single parents, blended families and all varieties of "alternative lifestyles," young people still often have extremely traditional ideas concerning relationships. The Stepfamilies Association of America has 22 definitions of what constitutes a family. A major goal of this chapter is to help them recognize what they probably already know on some level-that families today don't bear much resemblance to the old "Ozzie and Harriet" stereotypes. The way we live now requires certain adjustments both at home and on the job. The exercises in this chapter should help students make them.

Housework: See Yourself as Management, Not Always as Labor

PAGES 178-180 **Workbook 76-77**

Objective:

To show that it's not necessary for one person to take total responsibility for household tasks. Most require little skill or physical stamina and can be done by people of all ages and both sexes.

Presentation Suggestions:

Have students complete the exercise and follow with class discussion. Answers will necessarily be imprecise, but that is not important. What is important is that class members rethink some of these common tasks and come to a new understanding about whose "job" it is to take care of household tasks.

Follow-Up:

Discuss the list of alternatives for accomplishing household tasks on p. 180. Can the class come up with any others?

Some women feel they are giving up power within the household if they don't do their own dishes or wash their own floors. This is a myth, and these attitudes need to be discussed and dismissed.

Communicating: New Strategies for Dual-Income Households

PAGES 182-187 **Workbook 78-80**

Objective:

To encourage *androgynous communication* within both sexes and to illustrate that appropriate response is dependent on the situation, not on the sex of the respondent.

Presentation Suggestions:

You may need to review and define the twenty-eight characteristics listed, depending on your class. Then have students go through and circle those characteristics they think apply to themselves. Then, ask them to analyze whether those traits have been traditionally considered masculine, feminine, or either.

Emphasize that in reality, people of both sexes can and should exhibit traits from all three groups. Those traits usually termed masculine are more appropriate at work or in task-related activities. Those thought of as feminine are more appropriate for use in relationships.

To practice seeing how this works, have the class choose the most appropriate response in each of the examples provided in the next part of the exercise. This can be done on an individual basis, in small groups, or in class. Follow with a discussion of why the class made the choices it did. In most cases, the response from the list of feminine traits is most appropriate at home, the masculine response is most appropriate at work. If students don't like either response, you may ask them to write new ones.

Finally, students are asked to write their own responses. They might be similar to these:

Your spouse accidentally overdraws the family checking account.

Tactful: I know it's hard to remember every detail when you're as busy as you are. Maybe we should set aside a few minutes once a week to go over our finances.

Your bookkeeper accidentally overdraws the business checking account.

Assertive: Handling company finances is your major responsibility, and you will have to do a better job if you want to stay here.

Your spouse's attempt at fixing the toilet is not entirely successful.

Sympathetic: You must be frustrated. I know how hard you tried to make it work.

Your employee's report on the project you assigned to her is not acceptable.

Analytical: I think you misread some of the statistics. Let's discuss it and then you can redo the report.

You are tired of being criticized by your mother-in-law.

Sincere: It hurts me to hear you say things like that.

You are tired of being criticized by one of your clients.

Willing to risk: If you're not happy with my work, maybe I'm not the person you should be dealing with.

Follow-Up:

Ask the class which responses were more difficult to write. If they had more problems in work situations, explain a possible reason for that: Most work situations also involve relationships, so there is an inevitable overlap. In fact, it may be entirely appropriate to use the feminine traits in work relationships. The masculine traits, however, are almost always appropriate when dealing with a particular task at work. For example, you may want to give a forceful presentation, write an analytical report, set ambitious goals, or make an aggressive deal.

Caring for Relationships

PAGE 188 **Workbook 81**

Objective:

To emphasize that a good relationship takes time and that it is necessary to set aside a part of each day for your partner.

Presentation Suggestions:

Have each student complete his or her graph, being sure to put in a wedge of time to care for relationships.

Follow-Up:

In class discussion, compare the average amount of time female students allotted for relationships with the amount of time males set aside.

Chapter Ten

Children & Child Care:
Careful Planning Pays Off

More than any other human relationship, overwhelmingly more, motherhood means being instantly interruptible, responsive, responsible.
—Tillie Olsen

Before I got married I had six theories about bringing up children; now I have six children and no theories.
—John Wilmont
Earl of Rochester (1647-1680)

Chapter Ten

Since most women are now in the workforce and 90 percent of all women have had a child by the time they reach the age of 40, it is essential that students come to believe that they are likely to be working parents. Therefore they must think about which kind of child care is available, which child care is affordable, and which kind would be ideal. They also need to be aware of how a child can have an impact on their career or increase the amount of stress in their lives so that they can better plan how to deal with these things.

In presenting this chapter, also make it clear that parenting is not solely a woman's responsibility. Try to get the young men in class to participate fully. Be sure, too, to indicate that no one is *required* to have children. Many people lead full and satisfying lives without them.

Child Care: What's Your Ideal?

PAGE 194 **Workbook 82**

Objective:

To have students expand their thoughts about child care, examine their own values on the subject, and see how these values might necessarily play a role in career choice.

Presentation Suggestions:

Have the class complete the exercise and follow with group discussion.

Activities:

Divide the class into small groups and ask them to come up with as many creative solutions to child-care problems as they can. This is not only good practice for building creativity skills, but as many parents have already learned, the cost of available child care can make creative arrangements a real necessity.

Invite a child-care professional to discuss her/his job with the class.

As an entrepreneurial exercise, have groups of students develop a model for a new kind of child-care business that would make quality care more readily available to more people.

The Economics of Child Care

PAGES 195-196 **Workbook 83-84**

Objective:

To show how career choice and income level enhance or hinder child-care options as well as other facets of adult life.

Presentation Suggestions:

As students work through the exercise, they should see how John has very few options for child-care — in fact, he is probably going deeper into debt each month. Jacque has more choices, and Joya, who has carefully prepared for her career, has the most options of all.

Follow-Up:

Discuss the questions that follow the budgets. In particular, examine the idea of some type of cooperative arrangement among the three parents. For example, if they could hire someone to come to the apartment building to care for the three-year-olds all day and pick the older children up after school for $5.00 an hour, it would cost a total of $200 for a 40-hour week. Under this cooperative plan, the cost would be about $66 a week for each parent, much less than they could expect to pay for a similar service on their own.

Ask the class, too, to discuss whether all three parents should pay the same amount, or if there should be some kind of sliding scale based on income, so that John might pay less than the other parents.

In reply to the final question, students should understand how continuing their education, delaying pregnancy, and careful planning will help them be better parents in the future.

Take Control and Plan

PAGES 198-199 **Workbook 85**

Objective:

To illustrate that there are other creative ways to mix career and family that may be less expensive or less stressful, or that may allow parents to spend more time with their children.

Presentation Suggestions:

Have students think of as many other strategies as they can. Some possibilities:

- Have a widowed mother or mother-in-law move in and take some responsibility for child-care.
- Have a student live in the home in exchange for child-care or household duties.
- Prepare for a job that allows part-time work in the office, part-time work at home.
- Find a job that allows use of telecommunication with the office much of the time.

Activities:

Invite someone following one of the strategies to talk about the pros and cons of his/her situation.

Taking Time Out

More Choices

PAGE 199 **Workbook 86**

Objective:

To examine the issue of career ladders and to create an understanding of how working in a field with strong career ladders may make it more difficult to take time out for parenting.

Presentation Suggestions:

Have the class think of possible careers that meet requirements for income and flexibility, but that do not have strong career ladders. Some possibilities:

Veterinarian

Psychologist

Computer service technician

Auto mechanic

Electrician

Wallpaper hanger

Follow-Up:

Emphasize the need for workers to keep up with changes in their profession while they are out of the workforce. Things are changing quickly these days, and a few years off the job can truly set back someone who has not followed the technology and trends. Keeping up can mean reading the professional journals, maintaining memberships in professional organizations or contact with peers, taking classes or attending seminars, and so on.

Resources:

Working Woman Magazine

Working Mother Magazine

Savvy Magazine

Inc. Magazine

Full-Time Parenting?

PAGE 200 **Workbook 87**

Objective:

To have all students evaluate whether they are good candidates for full-time parenting, providing they have that option, and assuming they are capable of supporting themselves if necessary.

Presentation Suggestions:

Ask students to consider the list of statements and decide whether or not they agree with them. Being a full-time parent is appropriate for some people, and not at all suitable for others.

In addition to looking at this exercise, you might have class members think again about the categories in which they scored highest on the income expectation survey in Chapter Three. The best candidates for full-time parenting probably scored high in "helping others" or "unfortunate necessity." Those most interested in "purchasing power," "power and prestige" or "measure of success" are less likely candidates, unless they have other sources for their needs. People from the "freedom" and "security" categories could go either way, depending on how they define their terms.

Activities:

Invite one or more full-time parents to tell the class about the rewards and frustrations of their situations, how and why they made their decisions, and their plans for re-entering the paid or volunteer workforce. It would be particularly interesting to have a father who remains at home to care for the child/children, if you can find one.

chapter eleven

Your Own Strategic Plan
for Mixing Career & Family

There is only one success—to
be able to spend your life in
your own way.
—Ben Sweetland

If you don't know where you are
going, you will probably end up
somewhere else.

I think somehow we learn who
we really are and then live with
that decision.
—Eleanor Roosevelt

Chapter Eleven

In Chapter Eleven, everything comes together. This is a career research chapter that departs from the traditional model by asking students to consider such diverse elements as how they feel about success, their child-care values, and their income requirements.

The whole book has been leading up to this point. In the past, students may have been asked to think about their goals or how they want to take care of their children. Most have been asked what they want to be when they grow up. But few have received the guidance necessary to see how all these things are related. Perhaps, in the past, there was less need to merge all these facets of life.

We strongly believe that, from now on, career, family and life planning must be approached as a unit.

What Would Make You a Success?

PAGE 205 Workbook 88

Objective:

To have students consider the various facets of life in which it is possible to be successful, and think about their personal dreams or goals in each. (Often young men think of success solely in terms of money, while young women tend to define success in terms of relationships.)

Presentation Suggestions:

Hold a class discussion on the meanings of the terms "success" and "failure." Write the different definitions on the board in separate columns, one for the suggestions offered by males, one for those offered by females. Note the differences. Then have students complete the exercise individually.

Follow-Up:

Ask students to share ideas about areas in which they feel most successful in their own lives.

Clarifying Your Thoughts on Family Life

PAGES 206-207 **Workbook 89-90**

Objective:

To help students clarify their current values concerning family life and child care.

Presentation Suggestions:

Have students go through each question, choosing the answer that most clearly relates to their own thoughts about family life and child-care. If none of the statements provided matches their goals, ask them to write their own response. Then have class members go back and read all the statements to themselves to reinforce their impact. In our career research model, these beliefs will need to be considered along with all the more traditional facets of choosing a career.

Since each member of the class must make these decisions by him/herself, the exercise must be done individually.

Remind the class that responses may well change over time, and suggest that members retake this exercise at a future date.

Evaluating Your Financial Needs

PAGES 208-209 **Workbook 91-92**

Objective:

To have students come up with a dollar figure that would allow them to live comfortably with the family arrangement they just described for themselves.

Presentation Suggestions:

First have students turn back to Chapter Three and review the income expectation categories in which they scored highest. Ask them to list their two top categories in the spaces provided.

Then have them proceed to complete a sample budget that they think they would find adequate for their own future. Having written a number of budgets earlier in the book, students should be familiar with the process by now.

Follow-Up:

If more budgeting work is required, see Chapter Three of *Choices, Challenges,* or *Changes;* or see pp. 45-49 in the *Instructor's Guide.*

Investigating Possible Careers

PAGES 210-211 **Workbook 93-94**

Objective:

To help students gather career information following a traditional career research model.

Presentation Suggestions:

Although we have provided only one form, ask students to complete this model for at least three different careers in which they have some interest. Go through all the questions in class before students begin and, if necessary, explain what each item entails.

You might take the class to the library or career center for instruction on use of career research materials. Or bring some of the most often-used resources, such as the *Occupational Outlook Handbook* and *Dictionary of Occupational Titles* to class.

The exercise can be assigned as homework, or you can allow time for it to be completed in class.

Activities:

Have a career counselor speak to the class about requirements and opportunities within some of the fields researched by the class. Or, invite guest speakers now working in some of those career fields to talk about their jobs and how they manage to mix career and family life.

Resources:

Michelson, Maureen R., ed. *Women & Work: Photographs and Personal Writings.* Pasadena, California: NewSage Press, 1986.

Now Let's Focus on How This Career Meets Your Parenting Requirements

PAGES 212-213 **Workbook 95-96**

Objective:

To have students consider these questions about their potential career choice: How flexible is it? Does it pay well enough to support a family? Would it be possible to support a family by working less than full-time?

Presentation Suggestions:

This is an important addendum to the traditional career research model. It asks students to think about many of the issues already considered in the book before making their career choice. You may want to review some of these before having the class complete the exercise individually.

Follow-Up:

Once the students have completed this research, ask them to report their findings for each of the three careers. This shared information will be useful to the whole class.

Once students have identified careers that hold interest for them and also meet their personal requirements for mixing career and family, try to arrange "shadow experiences" with adults in the community who hold those jobs. The opportunity to follow a person through a workday is probably one of the best reinforcements you can offer a student. Consult *Career Choices: A Guide for Teens and Young Adults: Who Am I? What Do I Want? How Do I Get It?* by Mindy Bingham and Sandy Stryker for details on how to arrange a "shadowing" experience.

Getting There from Here

PAGES 214-215 **Workbook 97**

Objective:

To help students form their own action plan for meeting the goals they have set for themselves over the next decade.

Presentation Suggestions:

Ask students to formulate a goal: Where would they like to be or what would they like to have accomplished ten years from today? Have them enter that goal on the bottom lines of the chart. Then ask them to consider what they need to do between now and then if they hope to achieve this goal. Have class members write concrete steps they can take this year, next year, and so on in order to approach personal success in this area by year ten.

Review the goal-and objective-setting exercises in Chapter Four of *Choices* and *Challenges*, pp. 58-62 in this *Instructor's Guide*.

Follow-Up:

Have the students turn back to p. 21 and incorporate this plan into their time-line. If they currently don't have children, does this now change their parenting time table?

Ask students to share their new time-line and the reasons for any changes.

Bringing in Your Partner

PAGE 216 **No Workbook Page**

Objective:

To emphasize the importance of choosing a partner who shares student's values on child care and family life.

Presentation Suggestions:

Raising a family is infinitely easier when both partners have the same ideas about the way it should be done. Remind the class of this and ask them to make note for future reference. When a class member is seriously considering a mate, he or she should have the potential spouse take the exercise on pp. 206-207. Then the couple should compare answers and discuss.

Resources:

Lindsay, Jeanne. *Teenage Marriage: Coping With Reality.* Buena Park, CA: Morning Glory Press, 1988.

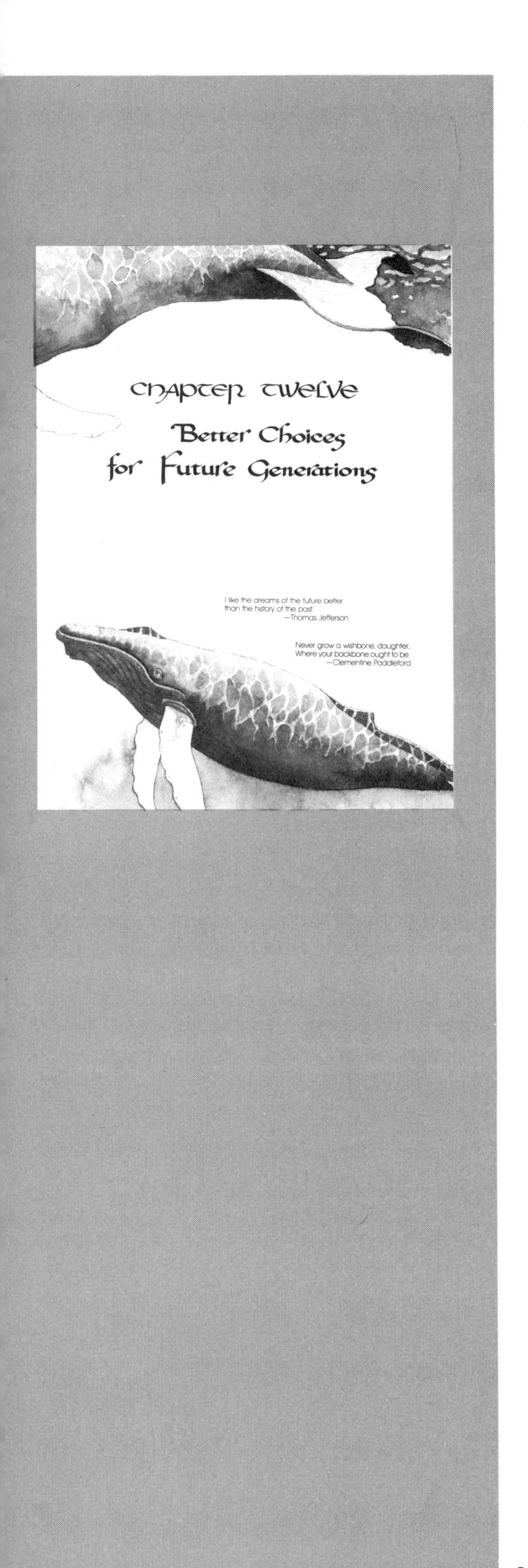

Chapter Twelve

This book is necessary, in part, because society has not noted nor acted upon the necessity for change in public and private policies related to family life. *More Choices* will help students work out better solutions for their own lives. At the same time, we realize that changes on a larger scale are long overdue. If they are to come about, none of us can afford to be concerned solely about our own welfare. We need to work together so that future families can have more and better choices for the way they live. This chapter is meant to encourage students to become actively involved in the process of change for their own satisfaction and for the benefit of all.

Authority and Power

PAGES 222-223 **Workbook 98-99**

Objective:

To link positions of authority with solutions to social problems.

Presentation Suggestions:

According to *Facts and Reflections on Careers for Today's Girls,* published by Girls, Incorporated, "By the fourth and fifth grades children are concerned about national and global problems such as hunger, poverty and nuclear war." It is important to "encourage girls as well as boys to think of themselves as future presidents, legislators, secretaries of agriculture, responsible corporate executives, nuclear engineers or religious leaders, who might have a significant role in bringing about solutions to these problems."

But many young women have ambivalent feelings about power and authority. They are not sure of their rights or their abilities to deal with significant issues. This exercise is meant to start students thinking about the positive aspects of power or leadership, as well as to encourage them to stretch their imaginations and make some kind of commitment to social change.

Ask students to complete the exercise. Follow with group discussion.

Follow-Up:

Divide the class into small groups of students who have the same goal (to be president of the United States, for example) or the same commitment (to world peace, a clean environment, feeding the hungry, and so forth) and let each group discuss what one individual could do to make things better for all.

Or, study the lives of individuals who have made significant contributions to society in recent decades. Some examples: Rachel Carson, Betty Friedan, Bob Geldof, Martin Luther King, Maggie Kuhn, Rosa Parks, Mother Teresa, Ralph Nader and Dr. Jonas Salk.

Resources:

Bingham, Mindy, and Penelope Paine. *My Way Sally*. Santa Barbara: Advocacy Press, 1988.

Authority and Power, Part II

PAGE 224 Workbook 98-99

Objective:

To show a logical progression from one job to another and to encourage students to think beyond the obvious entry level.

Presentation Suggestions:

This exercise could be particularly valuable to re-entry women by illustrating that, even though their current job may not offer much possibility for authority and power, there are natural steps to be taken that could eventually put them in leadership positions.

Ask students to think of logical job progressions for the entry-level positions listed. For example:

Child-care worker to preschool teacher to preschool director to owner of a chain of preschools.

Receptionist to secretary to administrative assistant to manager.

Legal secretary to paralegal to associate attorney to partner in a law firm.

Newspaper reporter to columnist to editor to city editor.

Follow-Up:

Ask the class to consider what training or education would be needed to pursue the progressions chosen.

Have students already working at an entry-level job consider how they could progress to a position of higher authority. Then ask them to consider educational steps they would need to take to reach each position.

Comparable Worth

PAGE 226 **Workbook 100**

Objective:

To let students employ their creative skills, social values and positive attitudes about authority in order to rethink the issue of comparable worth.

Presentation Suggestions:

Discuss the issue of comparable worth in class and then have students complete the exercise.

Follow-Up:

Ask students to take the position in favor of comparable worth and write a paragraph (as homework) describing the benefits it provides for each of the following: women, men, parents, employers, legislators, and day-care legislation.

Form a debate team to discuss the pros and cons of comparable worth. Then ask the rest of the class to form the jury and vote.

Resources:

Hewlett, Sylvia Ann. *The Lesser Life: The Myth of Women's Liberation.* New York: William Morrow & Company, Inc., 1986.

Maternity Leave

PAGE 227 Workbook 101

Objective:

To help students evaluate their own thoughts on maternity leave and consider what they might do to make life easier for working parents, if they were in a position of authority.

Presentation Suggestions:

Assign the exercise as homework. Precede or follow with group discussion.

Follow-Up:

Ask students to interview a working mother with an infant, or invite one to class to talk about hardships and problems and what might be done to make the situation better.

Ask the civics instructor to help you follow new legislation being proposed at the federal or state level.

A student interested in politics might want to give a speech on the history of this issue or make a comparison with other industrial countries.

Ask your local state representative or a representative from the League of Women Voters to speak to the class on one of these issues.

Child Care

PAGE 228 Workbook 102

Objective:

To encourage students to think beyond the obvious for solutions to the child-care dilemma.

Presentation Suggestions:

Ask students to complete the exercise and follow with group discussion.

Follow-Up:

Invite a panel of parents and child-care professionals to discuss their own desires for and concerns about child care. Ask students to pick one of the topics discussed in this chapter — power and authority, comparable worth, maternity leave, or child care — and write an essay on how this issue will affect his or her future career choices.

Lifelong Planning

PAGE 235 **Workbook 103**

Objective:

To encourage students to think about what they want out of life after child care is no longer a major concern.

Presentation Suggestions:

Ask students to turn back to p. 21 in Chapter One and note how many years of their life would not deal primarily with child care. What would they like to do with those years?

Some life-planning professionals now advocate serial roles — an individual might be a full-time student for a while, then perhaps a full-time worker, with years as a full-time parent to follow. When child care becomes less demanding, the individual might go back to school or take up a new career, a new cause, a new lifestyle. Discuss the pros and cons of this plan with the pros and cons of filling multiple roles at any one time.

Serial roles:

Place fewer demands on a person's time.

Require less action by employers or the government.

Require some other source of income during child-care years.

Are not realistic for people working in fields with strong career ladders.

Multiple roles:

Require more juggling of time.

May lead to positive action by government, employers or other household members.

Provide income when children are young.

Allow parents to advance in their careers at a steady pace.

Using More Choices in Various Settings

More Choices is a versatile tool that can be valuable in many different settings. These include:

Home Economics classes

Career Development/Life Planning classes

Single Mother/teen Parent classes

Math classes

English classes

Gifted Student programs

Vocational Readiness programs

Displaced Homemakers programs

Re-Entry programs

Parenting/Family Life programs

Drop-Out Prevention programs

Advising 4-H, Big Sisters, Girl Scout Programs

The following instructions show how *More Choices* can be used in a few of these settings.

HOME ECONOMICS/LIFE PLANNING/CAREER PLANNING CLASSES

This is the most obvious setting for the *More Choices* curriculum. Since the great majority of young men and women will combine family life with employment outside the home, they will desperately need the information this course provides. Getting it early, while they have yet to make important decisions in both spheres, improves their chances of mixing career and family successfully. Ideally, students should proceed to *More Choices* after completing the *Choices/Challenges* curriculum. More advanced or motivated students, however, may go directly to *More Choices*.

TEEN PREGNANCY PREVENTION AND DROPOUT PREVENTION PROGRAMS

A study by Michael Resnick and Robert Blum at the University of Minnesota determined that a major cause of teen pregnancy is NOT lack of sex education, but lack of understanding the of consequences of their actions. Teens need to be able to "project themselves into the future or understand that they have control over their own lives." Resnick and Blum go on to state, "It's clearly a developmental ability to be able to link actions now with consequences in the future. Kids are ultimately capable of making decisions. What's important is that they understand their own responsibility and the impact that decision will have on their lives."

More Choices can help. Exercises such as Melody's budget graphically illustrate the unpleasant realities young people are likely to encounter unless they stay in school and take personal responsibility for their lives. It offers help in developing the kinds of skills they will need to have control over their futures (the Five Cs of control). Then it encourages, motivates and shows them how to prepare for the kind of career that will allow them to live comfortably when they make a conscious decision to have a family.

GIFTED STUDENT PROGRAMS

Young women of high intelligence are still less likely than their male counterparts to enter the professions or prepare for a high-level career. Perhaps they do not receive the kind of encouragement at home and in school that boys do, or maybe there aren't yet enough role models for them to emulate. Many of these young women still believe that, while they may spend a few years in the workforce before they marry, the largest part of their lives will be spent in the home. (In a poll of the two brightest young women from every high school in one state, 93 percent thought they would work for five years or less!) *More Choices* can help these young women recognize their potential and motivate them to pursue their dreams by demonstrating that the careers they are quite capable of pursuing will also provide them with more options for parenting. Combined with the *Choices* curriculum, it provides a solid background in both career awareness and career planning.

MATH COURSES

Young people often shun math classes because they do not see math's relevance to their future lives. *More Choices* is filled with problems, exercises and graphs that involve math skills and, at the same time, motivate students to take advanced math classes throughout their academic careers. We suggest that math teachers take time at the beginning of the school year to go through the *More Choices* curriculum, paying special attention to these exercises:

Motherhood Is a Lifetime Job, pp. 20-21

Which World Do You Live in?, pp. 26-28

Realities #1, 2 and 3, pp. 29-36

Melody's Budget, pp. 43-46

Time — Your Finite Resource, pp. 65-66

Time and the Single Parent, p. 67

Time Is Money, pp. 67-71

Being a Parent Is a Job, Too, pp. 72-76

Professions, pp. 80-81

The Wage Gap, pp. 107-110

Conduct a Personal Survey, pp. 114-115

Vocational Education, the Best-Kept Secret, pp. 118-119

The Importance of Math, p. 140

Attitude = Success, p. 141

Getting in Shape for Math Success, p. 142

Math — The Critical Filter, p. 143

A Word Problem, pp. 144-147

Balancing Your Life, pp. 156-162

Prioritizing, pp. 163-168

The Economics of Child Care, pp. 195-196

Evaluating Your Financial Needs, pp. 208-209

Investigating Possible Careers, pp. 210-213

Getting There from Here, p. 214

This small investment in time in a math class will pay tremendous dividends in motivation for math during the remainder of the student's educational career.

ENGLISH CLASSES

Like *Choices* and *Challenges, More Choices* offers many opportunities to develop and improve communication skills. See p. 114 of this *Instructor's Guide* for ideas. Also an instructor's guide is available for use with *Career Choices* in core curriculum English classes.

RE-ENTRY PROGRAMS

Many adult women still do not recognize the possibilities or benefits of preparing for a career that will allow them to live comfortably on their own income. The *More Choices* curriculum can be a valuable motivational tool for use with re-entry women — especially those of child-bearing age or those with children still at home. It is a good follow-up curriculum for these women once they have completed the *Changes* material.

Resources

Ten Ways to Facilitate the Use of These Books in Your School and Community

Perhaps you are uncertain how to best utilize the *Choices* series in your school or community. Th
following may answer some of your questions.

WHAT CAN YOU DO WHEN . . .

. . . . your school administration is able to provide the teaching staff but has no funds for th workbooks?

Community groups such as Rotary, Soroptimists, Kiwanis, and Lions are often interested in providin funds for specific items/materials for youth. Requests should be in the form of a letter. If you know club member, have him/her lobby for you. Offer to give a presentation to the club and show sampl of the books and how they are used. A listing of local service groups is usually available from th Chamber of Commerce.

If no such group exists, or if none is able to help, sometimes a local business will support a speci project. Some will expect news coverage for their support. This is a form of advertising and publi relations for the business.

Your school's PTA may be willing to hold a fund-raising event. Find out who is the president an make a request.

If your community has a Girls Incorporated (formerly Girls Club) meet the executive director an program director and see if they might provide books as part of their teen programming.

. . . . your school administration loves the program but needs funds to pay for instructors an workbooks?

Instructors and books will require a more substantial donation. You should check on the legality c using private funds for a teacher's salary. If there should be a problem, determine other ways to mak such a gift to your school.

Will local foundations and clubs accept applications for funds from public schools? If not, possibly local non-profit organization working with youth could apply on your behalf. The organization wi lend credibility to the project and may even wish to oversee its effectiveness. The local library ma be able to help you determine which foundations would be appropriate.

. . . . your response is so good for the class that you will need an aide and none is available?

Once again, local groups are often looking for ways to support youth. Find a volunteer to make nine-week commitment. The Junior League can identify appropriate volunteers. Is there a voluntee bureau in your community? A local university or college may supply students who need placement o an internship. Your PTA may know of a parent who could help.

. . . . you can offer the class and provide the books but you need funds for transportation for field trips?

Decide how much it will cost to go to the desired locations and how many students will be attending. Design a fund-raiser with your students. Can each student make a contribution? Ask a local transport company to subsidize the trips.

. . . . your school district will permit a credit class outside the regular curriculum but you need funds to hire an accredited teacher and a place to hold the class?

First check for available rooms at your school, or check churches, local clubs, city facilities, and so forth. Approach local groups that may agree to sponsor a class. Determine just how much money you will need. The students may be willing to pay for their own books. Stress the value of the course and the special opportunity that this course provides for youth in your community.

. . . . you are enthusiastic about the concept behind the books but you need to excite others through a workshop or presentation?

Contact Advocacy Press and request the director of training. A presentation can be arranged for a fee. It will help to know how many people will attend and where it could be held.

. . . . you think that the books could be used in your school but someone would need in-depth training in order to become the instructor?

Training workshops are offered. Write to Advocacy Press for information.

. . . . you need to know what other schools and organizations have already successfully used Choices and Challenges?

Write to Advocacy Press and request the lists of schools currently using the curriculum and organizations that have implemented the program.

. . . . some courses in your school already cover some of the topics in the books?

The curriculum can be incorporated into many existing courses. The books are visually attractive and have proved very interesting to students. Check your school's career education program, vocational education, home economics, or family life classes, counseling program and rainy day curricula. The books are excellent for independent studies courses or extra credit programs, home teaching, or young mother projects.

. . . . your school district is not interested in a class but you think it could be offered as a teen program in your community?

Call Advocacy Press about the national *Women Helping Girls with CHOICES* project. It details the steps to be taken to interest your community. Approach leaders of church youth groups, the YMCA, YWCA, Women's Club, Rainbows, 4-H, PTA, Girl Scouts, Boy Scouts, Girls Incorporated, or any other youth-serving organization. The following resource information will help you develop your plan.

Community Resources

For guest speakers, presentations, donations and ideas, the Yellow Pages of your local telephone directory are invaluable. If your community has a Chamber of Commerce, obtain a list of member businesses and corporations. Also request a list of local clubs and organizations. You may want to make a special effort to contact service organizations, which are already committed to serving their community and may be willing to assist you, too. Many are interested in taking on community projects that aid young people. Your need may be for funds to buy books or take a field trip, to have a speaker for the day, to have a volunteer aide, and the like.

Choices is an especially effective outreach and expansion tool for the development of co-sponsored programs with schools, women's organizations, girl/youth serving organizations, churches, and family and community centers. In particular, women's organizations are using it for advocacy purposes and have been extremely responsive and interested in sponsoring *Choices* activities. Those groups that have displayed a strong and active interest include American Association of University Women, Junior League, Business and Professional Women's Clubs, National Charity League, Zonta and Altrusa. For information on the location of any of these women's organizations, call your local Chamber of Commerce.

Most counties have commissions: Delinquency Prevention, Civil Service, Juvenile Justice, Commission on Women, Commission on Aging, and so forth, that may have resources you can use.

If you need specialists, your city may have a community services department. Local corporations and businesses will have specialists in many fields. If a business is large, it may have a public relations officer who is looking for ways to support the local community.

Girls Incorporated, Boys Clubs, YWCAS, YMCAS, Girls Scouts and Boy Scouts, and 4-H have many contacts and resources along with trained professional staffs.

Your school board members may be especially interested in this class since it teaches the "Fourth R," reality, in a most effective way. They have probably approved inclusion in the curriculum and may have been exposed to some of the media coverage. They may want to visit the class and would probably be delighted with an invitation to share information on their expertise.

Your local newspaper can highlight your school program. Check with your school's policies before you contact the paper and remember to have approval from parents if students' pictures are taken. Consult Advocacy Press' publication, *Women Helping Girls With CHOICES* for publicity outlines, time schedules, logos and brochure designs.

Don't overlook the students themselves. If you get them really interested, they will generate contacts — fathers, mothers, uncles, and so on — and add that special touch that comes with personal involvement.

Whatever it is you need, remember to ask *everyone.* From colleagues in the faculty lounge to the sales assistants at the store, you may obtain surprising kinds of help. So . . . talk about it!

How to Start a Project in Your School

To organize a *Choices/Challenges, More Choices,* or *Changes* program in your school, you will need funding and support. Read this section of this guide for information on possible funding sources for your project. Then identify the most appropriate school for the program, and the person within that school most likely to be supportive of your plan (the principal, a teacher, school board member, PTA official, for example).

THE PRESENTATION

Stress the following points in your presentation. They have proved to be particularly convincing.

The curriculum is a well-tested, widely endorsed program. The material is presented to students in an attractive, self-discovery fashion. Offering precareer awareness information, it will greatly enhance a student's ability to select the appropriate high school courses and to research potential careers.

- THE "FOURTH R" IN EDUCATION TODAY . . . The curriculum allows students to come to grips with the realities of adult work and family life. Exercises like the budget project in Chapter Three of *Choices/Challenges* allow students to envision the way they would like to live as adults. This exercise effectively answers the often-asked question, "Why am I in school?"
- BETTER SELF-AWARENESS . . . Students learn to identify who and what influence the way they think and come away with a better understanding of both themselves and the world. This awareness often leads students to raise their aspirations for education and future careers.
- LIFELONG SKILLS . . . The class teaches skills such as goal setting and decision making, skills that will benefit students throughout their lives. By demonstrating the difficult responsibilities of family life and allowing students to see the future consequences of present actions, it can be effective in teen pregnancy prevention.
- THE CRITICAL FILTER . . . The importance of math is highly stressed and becomes more evident to students as they plan for their economic futures. Young women, especially, often fail to grasp this fact and, therefore, effectively limit their future earning potentials, even though they have a 50 percent chance of being the sole support of their family at some point in their lives.
- I CAN DO IT . . . Students gain self-confidence as they learn how to gather information, explore the working world, obtain help for college or vocational training, and reach for their goals.
- A FLEXIBLE AND ADAPTABLE PROGRAM . . . The curricula fit into a variety of settings. Classes may be held once a week or every day. The program has been taught in six-week through year-long sessions, with the most popular formats being quarter and semester classes.

If you need more information, call Advocacy Press at (805) 962-2728.

At your proposal meeting, you will need to establish what funding is available to the school system. Even though there may be a great deal of interest in the program, there may be no funds for books and teacher training. If you need to raise money, call Advocacy Press for information and ideas.

Some of the places you might secure funding include:

- **A local charitable foundation** — Call Advocacy Press for a sample copy of a grant proposal and supporting documentation.
- **State or federal funds** — Call your local school district and request a meeting with the appropriate administrator who is familiar with the different educational grants in your area. Or call Advocacy Press for the name and number of your state Gender Equity Coordinator who administers this kind of federal funding.
- **Fund-raising** — See the publication *Women Helping Girls With CHOICES* for the planning of fundraising or call Advocacy Press for details.

In addition to funding, your organization may want to provide a coordinator for the class, help provide speakers, research visual aids, set up a career seminar or fair, organize field trips to local colleges, or set up a shadowing program.

In our experience, once the class has been offered, the school invariably adds it to the regular class schedule.

Getting Local Support for a Program

Every community has organizations that might be interested in sponsoring or supporting a *Choices/Challenges, Choices/Changes, or More Choices* program. Consider the following:

Girls Incorporated	YWCA/YMCA	Junior League
Boys & Girls Clubs	Business and Professional Women	Rotary Club
Girl Scouts and Boy Scouts	Churches & synagogues	Kiwanis
Big Sister/Big Brother Programs	PTA/PTO	Lions
4-H and Future Farmers of America	Soroptimists	Altrusa
National Charity League	American Association of University Women	

If you are a member of a community service organization that would like to collaborate with the local schools, you might consider the following outline as a starting point for your planning process.

STEP 1 — Call Advocacy Press, (805) 962-2728, preparatory to developing your project plan. Obtain copies of *Choices, Challenges, More Choices, Changes,* the *Instructor's Guide* and workbooks, and ask for a press packet and support materials to accompany your proposal.

See the publication *Women Helping Girls With CHOICES* for a complete guide to introducing the program to your community.

STEP 2 — Establish the need in your community schools for such a project. Ask your membership to approve the concept, to support your request to a funding source and to commit themselves to implementation and service as advocates and classroom resources. If you are working with a local Girls Incorporated, obtain its board's approval for collaboration.

STEP 3 — Identify the most appropriate high school to approach with your ideas and the key personnel with whom to talk (e.g., principal, teacher, dean). Identify other important people with whom to talk (e.g., school board members, PTA officers, possible teachers of such a course).

STEP 4 — Identify a local funding source and inquire about its interest in such an educational proposal. (Do not consider regional or national foundations as a foundation might then receive several identical proposals!)

STEP 5 — Plan and hold a meeting for key people from the identified school(s), your club, and, if applicable, your local Girls Incorporated. Make a presentation on the proposed project. Assume that the school will provide the teaching staff and that your club will fund the books/materials, coordinate the pilot project and provide classroom resources/guest speakers. (Your club could fund a Girls Incorporated staff person to coordinate the project.) Set a possible starting date. Classes are usually quarter courses, i.e., nine weeks. Ask for letters of commitment and support from school officials and others who will be involved.

STEP 6 — Write your funding proposal, or hold a fund-raiser. Call Advocacy Press at (805) 962-2728 for help with your budget preparation. Mail or deliver your proposal with letters of support to the funding source. Good luck!

Sample Goals and Objectives

For Collaboration Choices/Challenges Project

Sample Goals

To promote the need for a *Choices/Challenges* Project in the school.

To introduce and coordinate a *Choices/Challenges* Project course at ____________ High School for the ______________ school year.

To provide training for the course instructor.

To assist the instructor with resources for the course to include those of the community, Girls Incorporated., and the Girls Incorporated National Resource Center and/or of ________________ (our club/organization)

To evaluate the effectiveness of the course.

Sample Objectives

)bjectives for the Project Could Be:

To make a presentation on *Choices/Challenges* to the high school and/or the __________ School District Board of Trustees by __________ (date).

To obtain a written commitment from high school to include the proposed *Choices/Challenges* class by ____________ (date).

Obtain final approval from our club and members by _______________ (date).

To set up ________ classes serving ________ students for _______ weeks.

Send the proposed teacher to a Santa Barbara *Choices/Challenges* workshop, organize one locally, or provide training materials and resources by ___________ (date).

To meet weekly with the course teacher and school administration to determine resources needed.

To order ________ copies of each book by __________.

To order ________ copies of workbooks by __________.

To prepare ___________ news releases about the course at ___________ High School for local media.

To provide a sufficient number of speakers and arrange at least _____________ field trip(s) so the class will be exposed to the business world.

At the close of the school year, provide the school with a list of resources and mentors that would be useful in future years.

To provide ____________ written reports for school, district and elected officials apprising them of the activities and direction of the course.

To design a simple evaluation tool for students to use at the conclusion of the course to provide data and facts for evaluation of the entire project and its effectiveness.

Project Evaluation

Advocacy Press advises the following:

- student pre- and post-test.
- teacher/instructor evaluation questionnaire.
- a selection of press releases and magazine articles about the successful use of the *Choices and Challenges* curriculum.

Evaluation instruments were designed by Karen Spencer, Ph.D., Omaha, Nebraska.

Books by Advocacy Press

Making Choices: Life Skills for Adolescents, by Mary Halter and Barbara Fierro Lang. Softcover.

In a single volume, *Making Choices* introduces critical issues of the '90s . . . focuses on building technical skills . . . romotes effective parenting techniques . . . defines child development stages . . . identifies problems of abuse and neglect . . . teaches young people to evaluate, explore, and plan . . . spurs them to use personal strengths for positive social action . . . utilizes proven methods to reverse gender stereotyping . . . engages youth in meaningful dialogue about cultural, family, and personal values. *Making Choices* is a bold new educational tool for vocational and personal planning. Teaches responsibility while having fun.

Choices: A Teen Woman's Journal for Self-awareness and Personal Planning, by Mindy Bingham, Judy Edmondson and Sandy Stryker. Softcover, 240 pages.

Challenges: A Young Man's Journal for Self-awareness and Personal Planning, by Bingham, Edmondson and Stryker. Softcover, 240 pages.

Gifts every parent, grandparent and caring adult will want to give the teenagers in their lives. *Making Choices, Choices and Challenges address the myths and hard realities each teenager will face in entering adulthood. They contain thought-provoking exercises that prompt young people to think about their futures, develop quantitative goals, make sound decisions, assert themselves, and evaluate career options, marriage, child-rearing responsibilities and lifestyle budgeting.*

Consider using these books with *Changes* for a dynamic mother/daughter or mother/son experience.

More Choices: A Strategic Planning Guide for Mixing Career and Family, by Bingham and Stryker. Softcover, 240 pages.

Traditionally, career planning and planning for a family have been considered separately, as though there is no relationship between these two major spheres of life. *More Choices* takes a new approach and shows how, with proper planning, it is possible to support a family- and still find time to enjoy it. This is an ideal book for people about to choose a career, whether they are in high school, college, or at the re-entry level.

Changes: A Woman's Journal for Self-awareness and Personal Planning, by Mindy Bingham, Sandy Stryker and Judy Edmondson. Softcover, 240 pages.

In response to hundreds of requests, we have adapted our popular *Choices* curriculum for adult women. Maintaining *Choices*'s successful format and approach, *Changes* has updated examples, stories, issues and exercises of interest to women 18 years and older. *Changes* is ideal for re-entry programs, college career counseling . . . or combined with *Choices* for a dynamic mother/daughter program.

Mother-Daughter CHOICES: A Handbook for the Coordinator, by Mindy Bingham, William P. Sheehan and Lari Quinn. Softcover, 142 pages.

This complete guide enables any parent or youth leader to conduct the nationally-known Mother-Daughter CHOICES project. For six weeks, two hours a week, mothers and their sixth or seventh grade daughters explore the world of work, attitudes, budgeting, values, decision-making, assertive behavior and sexual pressure. This guide includes publicity, invitations, schedules, graduation certificates, and ideas to on how to prepare young girls for junior high school and a career choice.

Women Helping Girls With CHOICES: A Handbook for Community Service Organizations, by Mindy Bingham and Sandy Stryker. Softcover, 192 pages.

This guide details sample projects including job descriptions for committee members and project timelines. Sample grant requests will assist in raising money for projects and a comprehensive publicity section includes new releases, radio and TV spots, logos, and brochures.

Minou, by Mindy Bingham, illustrated by Itoko Maeno. Hardcover with dust jacket, full-color watercolor illustrations throughout, 64 pages.

This charming children's picture book about a cat in Paris introduces a life concept still, regrettably, missing from much of children's literature-the reality that everyone, especially young women, must be prepared to support themselves. It is everything a children's book should be . . . imaginative, beautiful *and meaningful.*

Father Gander Nursery Rhymes: The Equal Rhymes Amendment, by Father Gander. Hardcover with dust jacket, full-color illustrations throughout, 48 pages.

Without losing the charm, whimsy and melody of the original *Mother Goose* rhymes, each of Father Gander's delightful rhymes provides a positive message in which both sexes, all races and ages, and people with a myriad of handicaps interact naturally and successfully.

My Way Sally, by Mindy Bingham and Penelope Paine, illustrated by Itoko Maeno. Hardcover with dust jacket, full-color illustrations throughout, 48 pages. Winner of the 1989 Ben Franklin Award.

In *My Way Sally*, a clever and compassionate little foxhound decides to use her leadership abilities to make a change for the better. Too often, children tend to connect power with domination and corruption. This book counteracts video and television images that show a world in which power is manipulative and leadership is tarnished. Today's children will delight in the discovery that power and leadership can be positive forces leading to a safer, saner and more humane world.

Tonia the Tree, by Sandy Stryker, illustrated by Itoko Maeno. Hardcover with dust jacket, full-color illustrations throughout, 32 pages. Winner of the 1989 Friends of American Writers Award.

Tonia the tree cannot grow. She needs to be moved to a more nourishing site and, understandably, finds the prospect of change frightening. With the support of her forest friends, who convince her that growth and change are both necessary and exciting, Tonia becomes part of a new world of beauty and adventure. Written in rhyme and exquisitely illustrated.

Kylie's Song, by Patty Sheehan, illustrated by Itoko Maeno. Hardcover with dust jacket, full-color illustrations, 32 pages.

Kylie, a koala, is teased when she sings — koalas are not supposed to sing. With some friendly advice and role-modeling she is able to risk disfavor and learns to sing her own song. Soon all the forest animals delight in her songs.

Time for Horatio, by Penelope Paine and Maeno. 48 full color pages. Hardcover with dust jacket.

An abused kitten blossoms when adopted by the gentle son of a tour boat operator. The kitten tries to stop Big Ben in order to abolish "Mean Time" and create a kinder, gentler world. Itoko Maeno's illustrations create a magnificent tour of the Thames and the workings of Big Ben.

Shadow and the Ready Time, by Patty Sheehan and Maeno. 48 pages. Hardcover with dust jacket.

A loveable wolf pup, returned from captivity to the wild, learns how members of a wolf pack support, care for and cooperate with each other. She also learns that, to start her own family, she must wait for the ready time. Shadow's adventures charmingly project important lessons about parenting and family responsibility.

Mimi Takes Charge. Softcover, 48 full color pages.

Whether plunging into the sea or creating games to play in the dark, Mimi is a fearless explorer who revels most in her own capabilities and independence. These ten amusing adventures will delight child and adult alike.

Mimi Makes a Splash. Softcover, 48 full color pages.

As she goes about her busy days, Mimi delights in the magic of such ordinary activities as playing in the rain, doing the laundry and watering the flowers. Through her innocent eyes the wold becomes one big playground to explore and conquer!

Berta Benz and the Motorwagen, by Mindy Bingham, illustrated by Itoko Meano. Hardcover with dust jacket full color-illustrations, 48 pages.

In August 1888 Berta Benz and her two teenage sons made the first long distance journey in a gasoline-powered automobile. They did it without fuel, supplies or the consent of Herr Benz. Follow the true story of Berta Benz and her motorwagen through the German countryside.

Mother Nature Nursery Rhymes, by Mother Nature, illustrated by Itoko Maeno. Hardcover with dust jacket, full color illustrations, 32 pages.

Lessons learned in the nursery are lessons learned for life. As we move into the 21st century, nothing is more important than instilling a love of Mother Nature in the minds of those who will ultimately decide her fate. This environmentally sensitive book of rhymes introduce children to the concepts of conservations and ecology.

Nature's Wonderful World in Rhyme, by William Sheehan and Maeno. 32 pages. Hardcover with dust jacket.

Lauded by leading environmentalists and educators, these imaginative rhymes and beautiful illustrations can establish a lifelong love and respect for nature and its fragility in the hearts and minds of children. The comprehensive discussion guide aids meaningful sharing with caring adults.

Foodwork: Jobs in the Food Industry and How to Get Them, by Barbara Sims-Bell. 232 pages Softcover.

From the foreword by Julia Child: "*Foodwork* is an orderly arrangement of real-life stories about people who work with food — teachers, cooks, farmers, authors, scientists, inventors, business and marketing managers. The book is designed to help young people make career choices by defining available options, necessary skills, job search methods and suggested readings."

You can find these books at better bookstores. Or you may order them directly by contacting Advocacy Press, P.O. Box 236, Dept. A, Santa Barbara, California 93102. 1-(800) 676-1480, (805) 962-2728.

Workshop and Training Opportunities

Workshops are held each year in Santa Barbara. Call Advocacy Press for dates and registration information. These popular workshops fill early so make your reservation at least two months in advance. Certified trainers are also available to travel and conduct local workshops for school districts, organizations and conventions. For a trainer brochure, call Advocacy Press.

Each Workshop Provides:

- An overview of *Choices, Challenges, More Choices* and *Changes* (including history, background and philosophy of the project).
- A discussion of the critical issues that led to the development of the materials.
- An outline of the various ways in which the program is being implemented across the country.
- Step-by-step teaching instructions.
- Creative ideas for effective group activities.
- Visual presentations.
- Resource information assistance.

For more information and a brochure, contact:

Workshop Coordinator
Advocacy Press
P.O. Box 236
Santa Barbara, CA 93102
1-800-676-1480, (805) 962-2728

Audiovisual Materials

In our own training sessions, we use a number of excellent film strips and videos.

"Another Half" p. 35

"First Things First" p. 81

"Follow Your Dream" p. 60

"Gentle Angry People" p. 48

"Heroes and Strangers" p. 35

"It's O.K. to Say 'No Way!'" p. 81

"Killing Us Softly" p. 24

"Making Points" p. 20

"New Relations-A Film about Fathers and Sons" p. 35

"One Fine Day" p. 28

"Sandra, Zella, Dee and Claire: Four Women in Science" p. 23

"She's Nobody's Baby" p. 28

"Someone's in the Kitchen with Jamie" p. 23

"Still Killing Us Softly" p. 24

"Teenage Father" p. 80

"The Secret of the Sexes" p. 23

MAGAZINES AND CATALOGS

Choices

Money

Working Mother

Working Woman

Savvy

Real World

Inc.

Girls Incorporated National Resource Center

The Girls Incorporated National Resource Center (NRC), founded in 1981, is a repository of information on girls as well as the research, training and distribution arm of Girls Incorporated, (formerly Girls Clubs of America) of New York. Providing the link between theoretical research and practical application, the NRC is a unique clearinghouse of knowledge about girls' needs and concerns and the best programs to meet them.

The NRC is an invaluable resource and reference base for anyone interested in girls. You can contact the National Resource Center both by phone or in writing, 441 W. Michigan St., Indianapolis, IN 46202, (317) 634-7546. Each division of NRC has a specialist ready to work with you.

Research Division

The NRC is engaged in action research to develop, refine and evaluate programs that are effective in meeting girls' needs. Focus areas include pregnancy prevention, science and math education, and sports participation. In addition, the staff collects, analyzes, reports and publishes research on girls and young women for use by professionals working with girls.

Library/Information Division

The NCR collection contains over 5,000 monographs, studies, texts, films, filmstrips, cassettes, videotapes and periodicals relating to girls. In addition, the center has an extensive collection of newsletters, research files of published articles, conference proceedings and statistical data. Also available are program models gathered from Girls Incorporated, agencies, schools, and youth-serving organizations. Of special interest is information on:

adolescent development

health and fitness education

single-sex environments

adolescent sexuality

juvenile justice

sports and recreation

gender roles and relationships

career development and employment

math, science and new technology

The Center responds to requests for information from Girls Incorporated staff and board members, schools and universities, the media, policy makers, parents and others who need to know about girls.

Publications of special note are listed below. For additional Girls Incorporated offerings, call (317) 634-7546 or write to the Girls Incorporated National Resource Center, 441 W. Michigan St., Indianapolis, IN 46202 for a publications list.

Facts and Reflections on Careers for Today's Girls

This book summarizes current studies and research on girls' futures in the workforce. It combines hard-hitting analysis of current and future trends with highly useful information for teachers, parents, youth workers and others interested in ensuring that girls can discover and reach their true potential (59 pages). $6.95

Facts and Reflections on Female Adolescent Sexuality

Ideal as a supplementary text or resource guide, this well-organized survey of current research promotes an understanding of the way girls develop. Important facts on teenage sexual activity, pregnancy and parenthood make this publication an important tool for program development (24 pages). $3.95

What Do We Know about Girls?

This transcription of seminar proceedings provides an in-depth look from researchers and practitioners on what is known about girls, what needs to be known, and how to fill the gaps (26 pages). $4.95

Youth & Society

A special issue of the quarterly *Youth and Society* that contains a comprehensive review of what young girls learn-or fail to learn-about careers. Articles include childhood influences on career choice; girls and vocational education; career awareness and planning; curriculum development; and many others. Published by Sage Publications, 275 S. Beverly Dr., Beverly Hills, CA 90212, March 1985 (130 pages). $6.95

WEAA – Women's Educational Equity Act Publishing Center

Since 1977, the Education Development Center (EDC), under contract to the U.S. Department of Education, has operated the Women's Educational Equity Act (WEEA) Publishing Center. The center reviews, publishes and distributes throughout the country a broad range of print and audiovisual materials developed under grants from the WEAA Program to promote educational equity for girls and women. Over 250 products available at cost through the center include curriculum materials for use in school systems; teacher training, counselor education and in-service staff development programs; educational policy and administration handbooks for K-12 and post-secondary institutions; and informational materials and career development workshop guides for specific minority groups, displaced homemakers, ex-offenders, and low-income and rural women. A free catalogue is available and the center also provides technical assistance in selecting materials through a toll-free line. Call 800-225-3088 or (within Massachusetts) (617) 969-7100.

Grading and Activities

With the emphasis on participation and critical thinking, grades and tests should not distract from th main purpose of helping students learn as much about themselves as possible. If you want or need t give tests, you might base them on some of the skills developed in the course, such as decision makin or goal setting. Or you might use some of the exercises in the book. These ideas, unfortunately, ar hard to get across in a true-or-false quiz.

Grades can be determined in a number of ways. Use a point system with points awarded for completin every exercise. Some exercises can be judged according to how thoroughly they have been done (lik research of a particular career). Others are either done or not done. Points can be assigned for clas participation, or, if attendance is a problem in your school, for being in class. Another method is t start each person with an "A." Points can be subtracted for behavior that breaks established classroon rules such as showing disrespect, not listening to others, or failure to participate or turn in assignments In other words, they can keep their "A" with enthusiasm class participation, respect toward others an involvement in projects.

Projects might include interviewing adults in various careers, keeping a journal, oral reports, panel and debates, career internships and individual research on assigned topics.

Our final exam asks students to complete a two-year plan. We divide the year into summer/schoo year. Students are asked to write two goals with objectives for each. For example:

Summer 1994 — Goal: Get a summer job.

1. Visit a career center and check job listings once a week starting in April.
2. By April 30 tell all my friends I'm looking for a job.
3. Make applications for jobs in at least four places by May 1.
4. Obtain interviews in at least four places by May 15.

The exercise is graded on how seriously it is completed, and how well the goals and objectives are written.

Anyone who participates in classroom activities and does the reading and homework should do very well.

About Teens

Adolescence is a crucial time in a person's life. This is when the transition from carefree childhood to responsible adulthood takes place. Individuals begin to become aware of their uniqueness and realize that they have particular likes and dislikes, talents, goals, and so on, unlike anyone else's. Adolescents normally feel a need to define themselves, seeking to know who they are and what they stand for. It is the period when the young adult wants to make a vocational decision and implement a plan for achieving this goal.

The profound changes adolescents experience physically and socially can be extremely confusing, often causing them to be uncertain about their roles. Such identity confusion can bring about feelings of isolation, emptiness, anxiety and indecision. Teens face important decisions that they often feel ill-equipped to make.

During identity confusion, adolescents may retreat to childishness as an alternative to the adult requirements they feel society is putting on them. Thus behavior is often inconsistent and unpredictable, and it's common for teens to vacillate between feeling like a child one minute and an adult the next.

The term "identity crisis" points to the necessity to resolve the confusion and form a stable identity. This crisis is an extremely powerful one, since the whole future of the individual may depend upon its resolution.

Adolescent cliques are another means by which teens defend themselves against identity confusion. Typically, the members of such a closed group dress alike and use the same "in" words, phrases and even inflections in their voices. Such cliques are highly exclusive, denying membership to anyone who does not meet the rigid specifications so highly valued by their members. By joining together in such a coalition, the adolescents are aiding each other in defining their identity by stereotyping themselves, their enemies and their ideals.

Adolescent love may also be seen as typically more a quest for identity validation than a sexual matter. As Erik Erickson observed, "To a considerable extent adolescent love is an attempt to arrive at a definition of one's identity by projecting one's diffused ego image on another and by seeing it thus reflected and gradually clarified. This is why so much of young love is conversation." (Erickson, Erik. *Childhood and Society*. New York: W. W. Horton, 1963)

Another extremely important part of establishing an identity in adolescence involves developing a coherent set of values. The young feel a need to figure out what they value and what they stand for. They want to know that they belong to a particular group, such as a religious or ethnic group, and that they are entitled to participate in all the customs or rituals unique to it.

Choices, Challenges, and *More Choices* are structured so that students will have a stronger sense of identity as a result of their active involvement in each chapter. By the time they have completed this journal, they will have clarified many of their values, set goals and formulated objectives to reach them. They will have had practice in decision making, identified skills they possess, and been given a good introduction to career planning. All of this provides a more informed, confident answer to the pervasive questions of adolescence: Who am I? What do I want out of life? How do I become a fully functioning adult?

Working with adolescents is an exciting, stimulating, and sometimes frustrating experience. We have included some tips for relating to teens that we have found useful.

TIPS FOR RELATING TO TEENS

1. Remember the names of the teens you teach. It is very important that you be interested in them enough to know their names and address them by name.
2. Point out to teens the cause and effect of their actions. Teach them how to do this for themselves on a short-term and long-term basis.
3. Before giving feedback to students, ask if they want to hear it. If so, make it as specific as possible and make sure the power stays with the students. Don't strip students of their self-respect.
4. Regardless of how much teens talk about how awful their parents are, never agree with them or make statements against the parents. Remember that their bond is very strong. This advice is just as true for siblings and friends.
5. Don't lecture to, or unload on, teens. You will lose their interest and respect if you do.
6. Teens often operate as if they are the center of the universe. This is a typical stance for this age.

   They are very much aware of themselves in every way. It can be beneficial if a teacher asks them to imagine how another person felt or feels in some situation. In other words, help them open up to the world of others.
7. Make good eye contact with your students, giving them your full attention.
8. To promote a feeling of camaraderie among the students and yourself, you may want to share a meal or a snack. This can be especially effective in "getting acquainted times" as well as for celebrations.
9. Use humor generously but appropriately when working with teens.
10. Open yourself to teens through as many channels as possible. This can be done by communicating how you are feeling and what you are thinking. It can be done by sharing humor, interests, and goals.

11. Be honest with them. Many of them see adults as two-faced. Don't do things behind their backs.

12. Expect teens to hold up their end of an agreement and tell them that you expect this. This gives them responsibility, power and autonomy.

13. Take a few minutes to be aware of your own feelings and concerns before you start the class. In this way, you are fully available to the students.

14. As a general rule, the teacher who is effective is cheerful, positive and relaxed. When you feel otherwise, share, with the students what has happened to produce your negative feelings so that they know they didn't cause them, and that your anger or unhappiness is not directed at them.

15. When a class period has been full of tension for an extended period of time, it is helpful to change the subject for a few minutes to relieve the pressure. A two-minute stretch break can be rejuvenating, too. Then return to the subject, remembering where you were in your conversation.

16. Low self-esteem is a common problem in troubled teens. You can help raise it in numerous ways. For example:

    a. Ask their opinion and really listen to it. Use their suggestions whenever possible regardless of how insignificant they may seem to you. They are important to the adolescent.

    b. Be alert for possibilities to create a private inside joke or secret you can share. This helps raise self-esteem.

    c. By your attitudes, words and actions, communicate to teens that you believe in them.

17. When talking to a teen who is especially frustrating or offensive to you, concentrate on something about him/her you do like, regardless of how insignificant it appears.

18. Help validate teens' identity by stating truthful facts about them such as:

    a. "You are more independent now that you are in junior high or high school."

    b. "You're developing more mature social, study, (or whatever is appropriate) skills now than you had a few years ago."

    c. "You are developing your own values."

    d. "You are beginning to wonder what your career will be when you are grown."

19. Expect teens to respond positively to topics in your teaching, and they probably will.

20. Be patient with teens. Accept their failures as necessary steps in learning to cope with life.

21. Admit your own mistakes. Let them see you as someone who is human and willing to change direction when you feel it is appropriate.

22. Be very clear about your rules for the classroom and just as clear about the consequences for students who stray from these rules. Enforce your rules by *action,* not by lots of threats, or blar It's always appropriate to express your anger, disappointment, or other negative feelings at thei *behavior* without damaging their sense of worth or dignity.

23. Be quick to express your satisfaction verbally or non-verbally. A pleased look, smile, and nod are great reinforcers, as are many positive statements.

24. Be especially alert to support and *like* the students who have the least going for them. You will earn the respect of all the students, the appreciation of the "under dog," and a priceless feeling of safety within your classroom.

Group Dynamics and Classroom Techniques

As a teacher, you will be working mainly in a classroom setting. It can be an exciting learning climate for any group. Groups can stimulate thought, be energizing, and provide opportunities for growth and development with less risk to an individual than in a one-on-one situation. As a classroom teacher, you deal with group situations every day and are readily aware of the positive and negative aspects of group interaction. In this section of your guide, we have included information and suggestions that can be applied to help group learning experiences be as effective and exciting as possible.

SIZE OF GROUPS

The size of a group affects the communication among its members. Although you have a specific group size to begin with, you can restructure the class into smaller units or groups for various purposes. Following is a brief discussion of different size groups along with the advantages and the type of activities suitable for each.

Dyads — Pairing students can help them become used to sharing information about themselves with others. Dyads are useful in breaking down "barriers" to communication. They can stimulate the sharing of personal opinions and ideas.

Trios — Groups of three are excellent vehicles for discussion. A trio is less intimate than a dyad, but creates a safe and efficient way to express a viewpoint or an idea, or to react to an exercise. Trios are very task oriented if the members are not close friends, a situation which may lead to excessive small talk and task avoidance. It's a good idea to rotate trio composition if closeness begins to interfere with the productivity of the group. The trio allows for both reporting to the larger group through a spokesperson and for some anonymity. It also provides a role for a vocal member as spokesperson and a role for a quiet or shy student as a recorder or observer.

Groups of Four or Five — When students gain more experience at communicating ideas and overcoming inhibitions, they are ready for a larger group. Groups of four or five are ideal for meeting sessions, making decisions and completing projects. Hearing oneself speak out in such a group, regardless of what is said, takes some risk. Dyads and trios are preferable until students develop more confidence. Learning how to meet and work on problems together is part of learning how to experience other viewpoints. Groups of four or five facilitate this kind of skill development well.

Groups of Six — When a group reaches six, problems of pairing can occur. In order for six to complete a task well, a leader has to be selected, preferably one with good communication skills. There is a tendency for a group of six to break down, fool around and avoid the task. The teacher can stop this by breaking the group into two trios, creating a spirit of competition between the two. This keeps the group focused upon the task. Groups of six are good for personal feedback. They are best used at the end of the course, if the focus is upon personal development and goals achieved.

Groups of Seven or More — Groups of seven or more decrease the probability for communication and task completion. They will be comfortable for people who don't want to participate actively, but who like to sit back and listen.

GROUP STRATEGIES: STRUCTURED EXPERIENCES WITHIN A GROUP

Many different techniques can be used in the classroom to provide interest and to allow for the most effective teaming mode for each topic. It is important to select the techniques that best match your teaching style and the needs of the students. This will vary according to class and topic. Be sure to allow enough time to complete a topic and to reflect on each exercise. This builds group teaming and cohesiveness.

Brainstorming — Members of the group contribute suggestions or ideas aloud as quickly as they can, without comment or criticism from the group.

Sometimes it is fun to have a "brain barrer" where the storm of ideas might be collected. One student can be selected to read the ideas. Then the ideas are put up on the chalkboard and analyzed to see which categories they fall into, or what the group feels are the most interesting or important.

The teacher can introduce the process by asking, "Think of as many ways to, or different aspects of . . . .

Buzz Group —This is a small reaction group that discusses some idea or concept.

This technique has been especially useful for groups of six or less to react to a question, or speaker or to come up with an opinion that will be shared with other groups. It is important to stimulate participation and competition by setting a time limit.

Case Studies —An example of an actual situation is analyzed. Case studies are often interesting to students and allow them to relate to a situation on a personal level. Students can be asked to write case studies from their experiences or find examples in newspapers or magazines to illustrate ideas.

Debate — Individuals or teams present and support opposing points of view on an issue or idea.

Debates allow differing points of view to be expressed and discussed. The audience may judge the merits of the arguments.

Dialogue —Two individuals take part in a conversation in front of the group.

No discussion should occur until the dialogue is completed. A lively discussion may follow, especially if the students speaking react first, indicating how they felt about their own argument.

Exercises — These are materials designed to stimulate thought and student response, usually in written form.

The heart of the books is their carefully developed exercises used to teach life skills. Exercises should be adapted to fit the needs of the group.

Fishbowl — A fishbowl is a discussion group of six or less who sit in a circle and discuss an issue or case study. The rest of the class watches and listens.

Interview — Students ask another person a series of questions.

Interviews with outside resource people encourage students to explore the attitudes of others.

Journals — Students record their thoughts, insights and reactions on any subject.

In the class the journals should be related to the concepts covered. To stimulate interest, it might be useful to read the journals of famous men and women.

Lecture — Information is presented through a speech.

Outside speakers can be used to clarify each topic and elaborate on a concept.

Models — Models present concrete illustrations of concepts, processes, or a sequence of events. They are a visual representation of a process.

Peer Learning Group — Peers are assigned to teams and lead exercises.

Training for peer leaders is important.

Role Playing — A situation is presented and individuals are asked to act out the roles.

Role playing can be scary because it elicits emotional material. If this method is used, it is important to ask the participants how they feel before and after the experience.

Skit — A group presents a play.

Skits should usually be practiced and prepared ahead of time.

STIMULATING PARTICIPATION WITHIN A GROUP — OVERCOMING PREDICTABLE PROBLEMS

We speak about using groups in teaching as if they were simple instruments for increasing involvemer and interest. In actuality, a group is a very complex device — and teachers soon discover that no tw are alike. To maximize individual participation within the group experience, the following element are essential:

The students want to learn.

The atmosphere is informal.

The examples and exercises are relevant and deal with problems to which the students can relate.

Students accept the challenge to have new experiences and to try new ways of learning.

When we speak of participation, we cannot avoid the subject of motivation. Motivation varies fron individual to individual, but we have found that many people are motivated by the involvement o others in solving a problem. They enjoy decision making within a group. A group offers opportunitie to generate many different ideas, viewpoints and experiences that one might not experience on one's own. Studies indicate that motivation directly affects teaming outcome. Also important is a commo finding that individuals are motivated by goal-directed behavior. Each chapter in the books sets clea learning objectives. If students know the goals and purpose of the material and it is tailored to thei interest, they tend to be more motivated than if the material is simply presented.

To enhance participation within the group experience, some predictable problems, along wit suggestions for dealing with them, are listed below.

Problems:	***Suggestions:***
"I can't get a word in. . . ."	Divide into pairs or teams.
	Ask each twosome to come up with the number of ideas you want. Take turns sharing these with the larger grour
"Someone already said my idea. . . .	Ask the student to restate the idea in his/her own words and elaborate on it.
"I'm too embarrassed." "Someone might laugh at me."	Students who are very self-conscious can be encouraged to communicate by using dyads or trios to help them fee safe. They can eventually be moved to larger groups.
	Give these students consistent encouragement by verbal and nonverbal means. Example of verbal: "Sue, you loo ready to begin." Nonverbal: Look at Sue and smile at whatever she adds, regardless of how insignificant it is.

"No one's serious.
They're not paying attention."

When students are tense, or trying to establish feelings of identification within a group, they may act rowdy to make themselves more comfortable and make the setting less formal.

The teacher needs to confront the problem in an open way by expressing how she/he feels with this going on. "When you don't pay attention, I feel really frustrated. I'd like to go back to more traditional lessons." Then listen to how the students respond. Or, "This is different, isn't it? It's risky to share personal experiences and feelings. What ideas do you have that would make this situation more comfortable for everyone?"

"I'm so bored. . . ."

Lack of motivation contributes to boredom. It is important to discover interest areas and goals of individual students to keep them involved. Boredom is usually related to lack of involvement. The group is probably too large if people are getting bored. Go to a smaller group.

Students may act bored when they don't understand the material. Clarify the assignment, watching to see if students look more alert and become involved. Ask students for ways they could make the material more interesting and use some of their suggestions.

"I can't seem to concentrate. . . ."

Physical health affects concentration, as does the level of fatigue. It may be helpful to take a stand-up break and allow for tension reduction. A group "energizer" exercise can be used to refresh interest and concentration. It's often helpful to ask students to close their eyes, relax and let their imagination take them to whatever situation is keeping them from concentration. Give two to three minutes to this exercise; then bring their attention back to the present, noticing what they see, hear, and feel physically. Such a grounding exercise promotes being fully in the present again.

"This is dumb!"
"I can't stand Johnny. . . ."

There are times when individuals need to resolve conflicts or bad feelings. Students have to be told to settle differences after the session. Moving people to different groups may reduce problems.

To respond to, "This is dumb," you might say, "Instead of criticizing, I'd like you to say exactly what you don't like and what you would like to see happen instead."

HOW EFFECTIVE ARE YOUR GROUPS?

We've included a checklist to help you analyze your groups. Review it periodically to assess you classroom experience. If some changes are indicated, review discussion guidelines and group techniques. Planning and evaluation are important elements to a successful program.

Checklist for an Effective Group Experience:

- Participation is shared and divided among members.
- Participation in group-stimulated thinking and involvement occur.
- Group completed the task.
- Group atmosphere was positive and friendly.
- Communication of ideas and feelings was accepted by members.
- Results accomplished are clear to all.

Bibliography

Andrews, Lori B. "Myths and Facts about Working Women." *Parents Magazine,* 58, July 1983, p. 26.

Baldwin, Deborah. "Women Helping Women." *Common Cause,* March/April 1983.

Bingham, Mindy, and Sandy Stryker. *More Choices: A Strategic Planning Guide for Mixing Career and Family.* Santa Barbara, CA: Advocacy Press, 1987.

Bingham, Mindy, and Sandy Stryker. *Career Choices: A Guide for Teens and Young Adults, Who Am I? What Do I Want? How Do I Get It?.* Santa Barbara, CA: Academic Innovations, 1990.

Bion, W. R. *Experience in Groups.* New York: Basic Books, 1959.

Bloom, Lynn Z., Karen Coburn, and Joan Pearlman. *The New Assertive Woman.* New York: Dell Publishing Co., Inc., 1975.

Bolles, Richard Nelson. *What Color Is Your Parachute?* Berkeley, CA: Ten Speed Press, 1989.

Broverman, Inge K., et al. "Sex Role Stereotypes and Clinical Judgements of Mental Health," *Journal of Consulting and Clinical Psychology,* 34, no. 1 (1970): pp.1-7.

Burack, Elmar H, Maryann Albrect, and Helen Settler. *A Woman's Guide to Career Satisfaction.* Belmont, CA: Wadsworth, Inc., 1980.

Butler, Pamela E. *Self-Assertion for Women.* San Francisco: Canfield Press, a division of Harper and Row, 1981.

Caron, Ann F. *Don't Stop Loving Me: A Reassuring Guide for Mothers of Adolescent Daughters.* New York: Henry Holt and Company, 1991.

Carson, Dale. *Girls Are Equal Too: The Women's Movement for Teenagers.* New York: Atheneum, 1973.

Comiskey, James. *How to Staff, Expand and Sell a Business: A Complete Guidebook for Entrepreneurs.* San Jose, CA: Venture Perspectives Press, 1985. (4300 Stevens Creek Blvd., Suite 155, San Jose, CA 95129)

Crystal, John C., and Richard Bolles. *Where Do I Go from Here with My Life?* Berkeley, CA: 1974.

Dowling, Collette. *The Cinderella Complex.* New York: Simon and Schuster, Inc., 1981.

Dryfoos, Joy G. "Strategies for Prevention of Adolescent Pregnancy: A Personal Quest." *Impact 83-84,* No. 6. Syracuse, New York: Official Publication of the Institute for Family Research and Education, Syracuse University, 1983-84 Edition.

Eastman, Raisa. *A Portrait of American Mothers & Daughters.* Pasadena: NewSage Press, 1986.

Erikson, Erik. *Childhood and Society*. New York: W. W. Norton, 1963.

Farley, Jennie, ed. *The Woman in Management Career and Family Issues*. New York: ILR Press, 1983.

Foster, Sallie. *One Girl in Ten: A Self-Portrait of the Teen-age Mother*. Claremont, CA: Arbor Press, 1981.

Friedan, Betty. "The Second Stage." *Redbook,* January 1980.

Friedman, Sonya. *Smart Cookies Don't Crumble*. New York: Pocket Books, 1985.

Friggens, Paul. "The Indispensable Man Is Only a Modern Myth." *Nation's Business*, 67, May 1979, p. 63.

Furstenberg, Frank F., Jr. *Unplanned Parenthood: The Social Consequences of Teenage Childbearing*. The Free Press 1979.

Future Homemakers of America. *Handbook for Youth Centered Leadership*. Reston, VA: Future Homemakers of America, 1982.

Gelatt, H. B., Barbara Varenhorst, and Richard Carey. *Deciding: A Leader's Guide*. New York: College Entrance Examination Board, 1972.

Goldberg, Herb. *The Hazards of Being Male*. New York: The New American Library, 1976.

Goldberg, Herb. *The New Male*. New York: The New American Library, 1979.

Golembiewski, R. T. *The Small Group*. Chicago: University of Chicago Press, 1962.

Gould, Lois. "X: A Fabulous Child's Story," *Women in the Year 2,000*. New York: Arbor House, 1974.

Hagener, Karen C. ed. *Peterson's: The College Money Handbook*. Princeton, NJ: Peterson's Guides, 1983.

Hewlett, Sylvia Ann. *A Lesser Life: The Myth of Women's Liberation in America*. New York: William Morrow & Co, 1986.

Hunt, Morgan. "Seven Steps to Better Thinking." *Readers Digest,* April 1983.

Jongeward, Dorothy, and Dru Scott. *Women As Winners*. Reading, MA: Addison-Wesley Publishing Company, 1976.

Kaseberg, Alice, Nancy Kreinberg, and Diane Downie. *Equals*. Berkeley, CA: Lawrence Hall of Science, 1980.

Keeslar, Oreon. *Financial Aids for Higher Education: A Catalogue for Undergraduates*. Dubuque, IA: Wm. C. Brown Publishers, 1984.

Knowles, M. and H. *Introduction to Group Dynamics*. Chicago: Association Press, Follett Publishing, 1972.

Kolbenscldag, Madonna. *Kiss Sleeping Beauty Good-bye*. New York: Bantam Books, 1979.

Kosterlitz, Julie, and Florence Graves. "Should Nurses Be Paid as Much as Truck Drivers?" Debate between Betty Friedan and Phyllis Schlafly." *Common Cause*. March/April 1983.

Lenz, Elinor, and Barbara Myerhoss. *The Feminization of America*. Los Angeles, CA: Jeremy P. Tarcher, Inc., 1985.

Lever, William Edward. *How to Obtain Money for College*. New York: Arco Publishing Company, Inc., 1978.

Lindsay, Jeanne. *Teenage Marriage: Coping With Reality*. Buena Park, CA: Morning Glory Press, 1988.

Lindsay, Jeanne and Sharon Rodine. *Teen Pregnancy Challenge: Strategies for Change, Book 1*. Buena Park, California: Morning Glory Press, 1989.

Lindsay, Jeanne and Sharon Rodine. *Teen Pregnancy Challenge: Programs for Kids, Book 2*. Buena Park, CA: Morning Glory Press, 1989.

"Mathematical Sex Differences — It's in The Numbers." *Science News,* 118, December 13, 1980, p. 372.

Mason, Mary A. *The Equality Trap: Why Women Are in Trouble at Home & at Work*. New York: Simon and Schuster, Inc., 1988.

McCullough, Joan. *First of All-Significant "Firsts" by American Women*. New York: Holt, Rinehart, and Winston, 1980.

McLaughlin, Steven D. *The Changing Lives of American Women*. Chapel Hill, North Carolina: University of North Carolina, 1988.

Michelson, Maureen R., ed. *Women & Work: Photographs and Personal Writings*, Pasadena: NewSage Press, 1986.

Naifek, Steven, and Gregory White Smith. *Why Can't Men Open Up?* New York: Clarkson N. Potter, 1984.

Naisbitt, John. *Megatrends*. New York: Warner Books, 1982.

Naisbitt, John. and Patricia Aburdene. *Re-inventing the Corporation*. New York: Warner Books, 1985.

Nicholson, Heather Johnston. *Facts and Reflections on Careers for Today's Girls*. Girls Inc. National Resource Center, 441 West Michigan Street, Indianapolis, IN 46202, 1985.

Occupational Outlook Handbook, 1990-1991 edition. U.S. Department of Labor—Bureau of Labor Statistics.

O'Neill, Lois Decker,ed. *The Women's Book of World Records and Achievements*. Information House Books, 1979.

O'Reilly, Jane. *The Girl I Left Behind.* New York: Macmillan Publishing Co., Inc., 1980.

Peterson's Four Year Colleges. Princeton, NJ: Peterson's Guides, 1984.

Pogrebin, Letty Cottin. *Stories for Free Children.* New York: McGraw Hill, 1982.

Racosky, Richard. *d + a=R: dreams + action=Reality.* Mount Clemens, Michigan: ActionGraphics Intl., 1988.

Ricci, Larry J. *High Paying Blue-Collar Jobs for Women.* New York: Ballantine Books, 1981.

Rogers, Carl B. *On Becoming a Person.* Boston: Houghton Mifflin, 1961.

Schaevitz, Marjorie Hansen. *The Superwoman Syndrome.* New York: Warner Books, 1984.

Schlafly, Phyllis, and Betty Friedan. "Face Off — Should Nurses Be Paid as Much as Truck Drivers?" *Common Cause* March/April 1983. pp. 36-39.

Scholz, Nelle Tumlin, Judith Sosebee Prince, and Gordon Porter Miller. *How To Decide: A Workbook for Women.* New York: Avon Books, 1978.

Simon, Sidney B., Leland W. Howe, and Howard Kirschenbaum. *Values Clarification: A Handbook for Teachers and Students,* revised ed. New York: A and W Publishers, Inc., 1972.

Skolnick,Joan, Carol Langbort and Lucille Day. *How to Encourage Girls in Math and Science: Strategies for Parents and Educators.* Palo Alto: Dale Seymour Publications, 1982.

Straughn, Charles, Barbarasue Lovejoy Straughn. *Lovejoy's College Guide.* New York: Monarch Press, 1988.

Tavris, Carol, with Alice I. Baumgartner. "How Would Your Life Be Different if You'd Been Born a Boy?" *Redbook,* February 1983.

Teenage Pregnancy: The Problem That Hasn't Gone Away. The Alan Guttmacher Institute. 360 Park Avenue South, New York, NY 10010, 1981.

Today's Girls - Tomorrow's Women. A National Seminar, June 13-15, 1978. Wingspread Conference Center: Racine, Wisconsin: 1979, updated 1980. Girls, Inc. National Resource Center, Indianapois, Indiana.

Vare, Ethlie and Oreg Ptochek. *Mothers of Invention: From the Bra to the Bomb and Thier Unforgettable Ideas.* New York: Quill WIlliam Morrow, 1987.

Viscott, David, M.D. *Risking.* New York., Pocket Books, 1979.

Women's Action Alliance. *Women's Action Almanac.* New York: William Morrow & Co., Inc., 1979

Wright, Barbara Drygulski, ed. *Women, Work and Technology*. Ann Arbor: The University of Michigan Press, 1990.

Wright, John W. *The American Almanac of Jobs and Salaries*, revised ed. New York: Avon Books, 1987.

About Authors and Trainers

Mindy Bingham

Intuitive and creative, Mindy Bingham provided the direction and energy needed to bring *Choices and Challenges* to life. Executive Director of the Girls Club of Santa Barbara since 1973, part-time college instructor and publisher of Advocacy Press, Mindy fulfills a lifelong dream with these books. She conceived the budget exercise while working with teenagers over twelve years ago and went on to develop a curriculum outline for *Choices*. Through years of work with girls, research and relying on her imagination, she created most of the exercises found in *Choices, Challenges, Changes, and More Choices*. As publisher, she coordinated the book design, art concepts, and marketing. She is also the author of *Minou,* a children's book and a Writer's Digest Bookclub main selection, *Is There a Book Inside You?* Her self-published book, *Career Choices: A Guide for Teens and Young Adults, Who Am I? What Do I Want? How Do I Get It?* was co-authored with Sandy Stryker.

Mindy, a California native, received a bachelor of science degree in Animal Science from California State Polytechnic University at Pomona. She lives with her daughter in Santa Barbara.

Sandy Stryker

Sandy Stryker is a coauthor of *Choices, Challenges, Changes, and More Choices*. A professional writer, she is particularly interested in issues affecting women of all ages. Her children's book, *Tonia the Tree*, won the Friends of America Writers Merit Award in 1989. She has been active in various service and political agencies, including the National Organization for Women, having served on the Minnesota state board. She holds a degree in Journalism from the University of Minnesota.

Penelope C. Paine

Penelope C. Paine is the Educational Services Director, Advocacy Press/Girls Inc. of Santa Barbara. Formerly Executive Director of Girls, Inc. of Carpinteria, California, she received a bachelor of arts degree from the University of London. She brings many years of experience in youth services to her presentations. She presents the workshop, *Choices and Challenges,* across the country to school administrators, teachers and counselors. She is an active community volunteer, especially interested in delinquency prevention and literacy. She is also co-author of the children's book, *My Way Sally*, which won the Ben Franklin Award for Best Illustrated Children's Book of 1989 and author of the children's book, *Time For Horatio.*

Linda V. Wagner

A nationally-known speaker and winner of numerous speaking awards, Linda graduated from Cal Poly, San Luis Obispo in Speech Communication and Journalism. Linda edits and updates workshop materials and publications for Advocacy Press. She is the National Coordinator of the Mother-Daughter CHOICES Project and travels nationwide presenting workshops to teenagers and adults.

Acknowledgments

The authors would like to thank some very special people whose efforts and assistance have been of great importance to this book.

First, we would like to thank Bill Sheehan who took the responsibility for turning the manuscript into a finished book. His hours of time in supervising the process and his contributions in both writing and design are truly appreciated.

Rose Margaret Braiden illustrated the cover and chapter title pages for *Choices,* about which we consistently hear rave reviews. We appreciate her contributions.

Robert Howard, also a talented artist, designed the cover and chapter title pages for *Challenges.* We appreciate his assistance.

Itoko Maeno provided the cover art for *More Choices,* and additional art work for pp. 9 and 97. She has contributed art for all the books and recognition for her work increases yearly.

Penny Paine added her expertise in the resource section of the manuscript and cheerfully listened to hours of music to find titles for our "Song of the Day."

In our "Tips for Relating to Teens" section, we would like to acknowledge suggestions from Gary Linker, therapist at the Human Relations Institute in Santa Barbara.

Christine Nolt, our book designer, deserves our highest admiration and appreciation for her untiring effort and her insistence on the highest standards.

And finally, we thank Chevron U.S.A., Inc., which provided financial assistance for our work.

We are particularly grateful to the many teachers who have shared their experiences with us. Specific credits appear throughout the guide, but many more have contributed through comments and suggestions. The overall enthusiasm has been overwhelming and extremely rewarding.

The authors